Caroline Rees

PAR GOLF
in 8 Steps

PAR GOLF

in 8 Steps

Joe Novak
Instructor
Bel Air Country Club
Los Angeles, California

New York **PRENTICE-HALL, INC.** 1950

To my wife

Edythe,

whose "direction" and "power"
have been invaluable to us in
the game of life.

Preface

HAVING USED THE METHODS DESCRIBED IN THIS BOOK IN showing hundreds of men, women, and youngsters how to score well consistently, I know that it will aid golfers in achieving skill in their favorite sport.

The book presents a simple, practical summary of the natural fundamentals of learning and playing the game of golf in the best possible manner as demonstrated by American professional golfers.

It isn't possible to name the many professionals who have made available to me, to their colleagues, and to all amateurs what they learned the hard way—trying to make good golf easy. I am, however, deeply indebted to them.

My thanks also to the members of the Professional Golfers Association of America for their help and encouragement.

I also want to express my appreciation to Tommy Box of Glendale for his aid as an expert photographer.

Joe Novak

Bel Air Country Club
Los Angeles, California

Contents

ix

Weight shift determines contact point in
swing . . . Why ball is played opposite left
heel . . . When to play ball opposite right
foot . . . How to Regulate Divots . . .
Chip shots . . . Cure for topping the ball
. . . The push shot . . . Sand trap shots
. . . Quick-rising shots . . . Hooks and
slices . . . Instinct vs system . . . Slices
. . . Why slicing is common . . . Cause of
shanking . . . How to slice . . . Stance for
slice . . . Procedure for Hook . . . Stance
for hook . . . Side-Hill Lies . . . Left-
Handed Golf . . . Common Faults and
Their Cures . . . Topping . . . Hitting be-
hind the ball . . . Slicing . . . Hooking
. . . Shanking.

"Warm Up" Thinking . . . A Lesson Each
Round . . . Organize shot-making thought
. . . Armour and Hogan . . . Basic Under-
standing of Actions . . . Macdonald Smith's
Method . . . Checking on the Swing . . .
Footwork . . . Differences between man-
nerisms, form . . . Physical Abnormalities
Misleading . . . Snead's own style . . .
Weight Transference Essential . . . Un-
derstanding the Fundamentals . . . Key
Movement of Footwork . . . Footwork
keeps head steady . . . Learn a Little at a
Time . . . Protect against confusion . . .
Golf practice not hard . . . Eight Steps
Are the Same . . . Swing simply organized
. . . Attitude for Learning . . . Pupil helps
himself . . . What's Hogan's Secret? . . .
Discovering and Curing a Fault . . . Eas-
ier learning routine . . . Why Young "Won-

1

Understanding the Golf Swing

Golf is the development of a spontaneous diversion of Scotch shepherds. It is essentially a simple, natural game.

Golf began when Scotch shepherds swung their crooks aimlessly at pebbles. Then came the idea of competition in hitting the pebble for distance. After that stage, some canny genius who probably was more accurate than long in hitting a pebble got the idea of competition in getting the pebble into a hole in the ground. From this combination of distance and accuracy requirements golf started.

Swinging the crook was instinctive to the shepherd. The first weapon and tool man used was a stick which served as an extension of his arm.

Ever since man first used a stick, his body has provided the power for the swing. Although his body position determined the general direction of his aim, his hands were the major factor in determining precision.

Only Two Elements

This primitive, natural combination of power from the body and direction from the hands is the basis of good golf today. The more simply these two essentials are combined, the easier, better, and more consistent is the scor-

1

ing. You can read books until your eyes blur and listen to advice until your ears ring, but fundamentally, good golf instruction means cutting out complications. The rest is embellishment.

Refinement and development of the game has brought confusion. The recognition and explanation of simplicity in excellent swings is difficult because so many see different features that they regard as the most significant points. Consequently, the more search there has been for the "secret" of golf, the more complicated have been the various interpretations of the "secret" which actually doesn't exist.

The only secret any great player has about his game is simplicity. Sam Snead, who has the finest swing in modern golf, makes no unnecessary or awkward motions. Ben Hogan was reputed to have a "secret" that accounted for his magnificent game. It was simply a move that he discovered was natural to him in getting in position properly for a most effective downswing. At the crests of their careers Harry Vardon, Bobby Jones, Walter Hagen, Tommy Armour, Joyce Wethered, Glenna Collett, Ralph Guldahl, Byron Nelson and other stars had no "gimmicks" in their swings; they hit the ball with the simplest and most natural swings they could achieve.

Every champion's game slumps when he passes the peak of natural simplicity in his swing. Whether the decline from this peak is physical or psychological—or both— doesn't matter. When a substitute for simplicity must be devised, the quality of the golf inevitably lowers.

The game is simple

The game of golf, as well as the golf swing, is simple in nature. There is only one basic rule of golf and that is, "play the ball as it lies." There are exceptions to this elemental rule, such as lost ball and unplayable lie, which are situations that have been associated with the game since its earliest verbal code was agreed upon. There also are more modern exceptions such as out-of-bounds and the interference of obstacles not in keeping with the fundamental character of the game.

The clubs, too, are essentially simple in character. There are only three basic types: The *wood* for "driving" the ball and getting distance; the *iron* for lofting the ball and the *putter* for rolling the ball.

A long swing is used for the longest shot within the range of the club, and a short swing for a short shot. That's simple; isn't it? The more clubs the player has within the reasonable, legal limit of 14, and the better fitted they are to the player's physical requirements, the easier the shots of varying distances, trajectories, and rolls and shots from the different lies. The objective of the clubmaker's genius is to simplify rather than to confuse, and to retain the essentially simple character of the game.

Despite the many evidences of the fundamental simplicity of golf, it seems that a large part of the mental and physical effort in the game has been devoted to making it complex. We make easy golf difficult by not understanding its simplicity.

The science of simplicity

Most of us would be excellent golfers if we could apply Plato's observation that beauty of style, harmony, grace, and good rhythm depend on simplicity. In our search for the solid foundation of simplicity in our golf swing, we experiment with what we hope will be the one great, right answer. When that answer isn't simple, we console ourselves with the reflection of an ardent golfer, David R. Forgan: "It is a science—the study of a lifetime, in which you may exhaust yourself but never your subject."

As a young professional it didn't take me long to see

that my pupils were not going to exhaust themselves taking lessons. They quit me long before that. And, as I became more experienced in teaching and playing, it grew increasingly clear to me that to be successful in my work I had to show results to the pupil long before he began to feel exhausted. Exhaustion at golf is for the professionals; we get paid for it.

The golf professional has the task of fitting a basically simple game to people who no longer are accustomed to simplicity. Youngsters can be taught a sound golf swing by being shown how to hold the club properly, then encouraged to employ instinctive actions. In many cases, a youngster picks up a pretty fair game without formal instruction.

A boy or girl acquires the knack of good golf by hitting the ball the easiest and most graceful way. If the youngster is inclined to be clumsy—and a lot of children seem to be—an instinct for imitation fortunately corrects this defect when the youngster gets an opportunity to see a professional with a good swing.

This is the factor that has accounted for so many caddies developing into good golfers. They subconsciously imitate the professionals at the clubs where they caddy. When "the pro" has a sound swing, the youngsters acquire it without conscious effort. And a bad swing by a professional or parent also leaves its mark on the naturally imitative child.

Teaching Older Muscles

The majority of the golf professionals' students are men and women past the age of quick and controlled response to muscle tutoring and imitation. However, the pros have done quite well in the difficult work of teaching this class of pupil who is utterly beyond the capacities of instructors in other sports.

The problem of instructing older people accounts for the growth of many varied and contradictory ideas about the golf swing. Every professional must contend with undoing awkwardness and habitual but unnatural motions that distort the adult's efforts from an easy, natural swing.

Golf instruction is further complicated because the professional is often in the situation of a doctor whose patient insists on a new pill when the first one doesn't cure him immediately. And because the professional always is trying to please "the patient," he may feel compelled to search for magic rather than simplification.

Tommy Armour had the right answer when, in his characteristically frank manner, he talked with a woman who intended to take lessons from him.

"How much will one lesson cost me?" she asked.

Tommy told her.

"And how much will six lessons cost?"

Armour told her the price would be six times the cost of one lesson.

Not discouraged, the bargaining woman asked, "Well, how much will 18 lessons be?"

Armour stopped her.

"My dear lady," he said, "I don't know that much golf!"

This confession, by one of the greatest players and teachers of the game, points to the experienced professional's realization of the fundamental simplicity of the game.

American Plan of Golf

The American wants a simple and complete answer to good golf. Life is faster and more crowded here than when golf instruction began in tranquil, Victorian Britain. The improvements in clubs and balls also has altered the playing and instruction plan.

The American plan of playing now dominates the golf

world. Scoring by the specialists who devised and developed the American plan has set a constantly improving standard.

The independent brains and diligence of hundreds of able golf professionals account for the development of an American plan of teaching that is comparable with the advance made in the American plan of playing.

There has been nothing different in the playing methods of Hogan, Nelson, Snead, Middlecoff, Mangrum, Demaret, Jones, Hagen, and Sarazen or Glenna Collett, Patty Berg, Louise Suggs, and Mildred Zaharias. Logically, then, the elements common to these superior American swings must be the foundation of the American plan of golf instruction.

Two influences retarded the development of an American plan of instruction. One influence, which has almost vanished, is the old idea of rolling the forearms (the pronation method) as the ball is hit. This was brought over by the early Scotch and English professionals. I've never been able to learn the reason for this action from any of them. It requires exceptionally fine muscular coordination.

This detail of the old swing has been virtually eliminated by the American plan of play, although Bobby Locke shows it slightly in his effective swing.

The other influence that delayed agreement on an American plan of instruction was endeavoring to correct faults in golf swings by trying to teach "feel" to pupils deficient in muscle and nerve responsiveness.

Routine instead of "feel"

The professional or expert amateur can learn to correct faults by recommendations which call for a nicety of "feel," but the typical golfer cannot. He doesn't know how he should feel in moving the body and the hands.

Only after long study of my difficulties in trying to teach "feel," and hours of discussion with other professionals concerning their troubles with this problem, did I discover that a sound platform of American golf instruction could be established by a routine of positions, rather than by vague references to "feel."

For more than 30 years I have been playing and teaching golf. I spent the first ten years in applying the experiments and conclusions of others to my own game and to the instruction of my pupils. My second ten years were devoted to appraising what I'd learned about playing and teaching and to developing a teaching procedure based on what the star and the typical golfer could do that would be identical in method. This procedure would have to give the typical golfer results closer to those achieved by the more physically fit and more diligent professional or amateur experts.

I had found that golfers were making the game too hard for themselves. I also was beginning to see that a plan of instruction such as is used in teaching the three R's or the piano or violin would make my teaching work easier and more effective.

"Mechanics" of the golfer

I had many discussions with doctors who explained bone, muscle, and nerve "mechanics" to me and this information always has figured prominently in evaluating observations of playing form in golf.

This emphasis on the "mechanics" of the golfer accounts for my formulation of a method of instruction that is different in some ways from the common ones.

The features of my American-plan instruction do not differ fundamentally from golf as it is played by experts. My American plan differs from methods of other successful teachers mainly in details of analysis or explanation.

The fundamentals of playing haven't changed since the invention of the rubber-cored ball. Improved play and much greater consistency in scoring has resulted from informed application of the fundamentals.

In golf instruction different instructors have seen different features. Their interpretation and explanation of these features have varied widely. But generally, the men whom I regard as among our great instructors agree on a few common denominators in a sound golf swing. These points, common to all good swings, have made me certain that the chief problem in effective teaching is that of making it simple routine for the ordinary golfer to perform the fundamental actions that expert has mastered.

In the refinements built upon these fundamentals, and in physical and temperamental qualifications, the ordinary golfer never will approach the star. The average player won't—or can't—spend time in making the fundamentals proof against carelessness, nor can the ordinary golfer devote the effort required to put a polish on his game. But, in acquiring the fundamentals as simple and sound routine, the ordinary golfer is bound to improve tremendously.

In having a simple, understandable plan—a plain, compact formula—the typical golfer can easily organize his swing properly.

By knowing the few essential components of all good golf shots, the player releases himself from the bewilderment that makes easy golf so hard. When he knows the few things that must be done, and the proper order of doing them, he protects himself against the lack of confidence that makes almost every shot an experiment to the typical golfer.

ORGANIZING YOUR SWING

By organizing his golf swing with my simple American-style routine, a player can practice with effectiveness and make the proper procedure habitual. The numbered routine further provides logical protection against the average player's game "going to pieces" and getting worse and worse as he makes wild guesses at correction or tries to heed the advice of equally uninformed friends. All the player has to do with this American-style routine is make his next shot strictly "by the numbers" and he'll find that he has been omitting some detail that accounted for his bad shot.

By using a routine of vital elements in the swing as a check-up, the average player can evaluate his efforts, understand what progress he is making, and know the details in which he is deficient.

Without reservation, I acknowledge my indebtedness to hundreds of professional teaching experts whose own experiences and observations have been freely presented to me for my work in arriving at a distinctively American golf form. In this book on the American plan are presented the teaching principles of my Professional Golfers' Association colleagues too numerous to mention individually.

The professional playing stars also have been thoroughly cooperative. In the third decade of my professional golf career, I spent a good deal of time at tournaments testing my research and theories. I rated the styles of the players according to the principles I felt were basic. In comparatively few instances did the performances of the players in competition vary much from the ratings I had made early in the competitions.

Learning by "Positions"

While I was making progress in determining the routine of positions that could improve on the "feel" theory of golf instruction, other professionals also were discovering that the numbering and positioning idea was effective.

One of the earliest I call to mind is Jack Fox, professional at a New Jersey club who was teaching "by the numbers," adapting the method he learned while a drill sergeant in the British army. Jack's daughter, Catherine, was among those he developed into excellent golfers by this method.

Johnny Revolta, whose mastery of the short game is outstanding, developed his "one, two, three, SWING" formula and uses it with decided effectiveness in his teaching. Wayne Timberman, whose juvenile classes at his club in Indianapolis have developed excellent golfers among seven- to seventeen-year-old boys and girls, teaches the youngsters by the numbers.

Other teachers and players have "counts" they use in teaching or in hitting shots. Helen Hicks had "oomPAH" as her magic word and had it stamped on the back of her woods to give her a rhythm of slow back and an accelerating, fast downswing. One of my pupils uses the phrase "Sell Spring Wheat" to time his swing.

Some instruction has been done to recorded musical accompaniment—the notion being that rhythm is the primary requirement. This is a case, to my belief, of placing the cart before the horse. With positions determined in proper routine, rhythm will follow almost spontaneously and will be governed by the player's natural tempo. Some will have very slow backswings, while others will have fairly fast but smooth backswings. All of them, however, must have downswings that speed up until the maximum clubhead speed is attained when the ball is hit.

Determination of the positions and the routine in the American plan is confirmed by countless hours of study by the great American players. This study has been of the players in actual performance and in motion pictures.

Only in a few cases have I found that alteration of the American-plan procedure occurs and then it is compensated for by a move, or moves, which have become habitual with the expert but call for fineness of coordination beyond the capacity of the average golfer.

Adjustments of fundamentals

For instance, Gene Sarazen at his prime had no noticeable forward press, hence no following slight slide of the body away from the ball in beginning his backswing. He picked up the club, swung his body around, then larruped the ball. But in his waggle he had a hand-positioning routine that gave him proper club face-setting before he swung. With the forward press, there is a natural cocking of the wrist by most experts. Sarazen simply cocked his wrists without a noticeable forward press and swung fast.

Vic Ghezzi—and to a lesser extent, Jim Ferrier—omitted coming back from the forward press before their bodies turned, but compensated for this omission by a body action the ordinary golfer would have difficulty in emulating. Ferrier, when he won the Professional Golfers' Association championship in 1947, displayed perfect footwork. He was really "on his game."

Some swing fundamentals

An impressive thing about the American plan of golf, to the rather inexperienced observer, is that it reveals virtually identical basic performance by players who seem to vary as much in style as Sam Snead and Paul Runyan. Runyan's moves in the routine were exaggerated, but in body and hand action he did, fundamentally, just what the other stars did, and the results paid off, especially in his defeat of such proficient and strong golfers as Craig Wood and Sam Snead for PGA titles.

Golf by the American plan does not call for different swings by players of different builds, or different swings for different clubs.

The swing of the woods and irons is the same in body action, footwork, and hand action. It's the construction of the clubs—different lengths, lies, and lofts—that accounts for the differences in positioning the body closer to the ball at address and for differences in trajectories of the shots.

Notwithstanding the confusion, arguments, and experiments about putting, the technique of putting does not differ fundamentally from that of other, longer shots. The mistaken attempt to keep the body out of putting has accounted more than any other physical factor for the uncertainty of putting.

The experts of 30 to 50 years ago, putting on greens that couldn't compare with today's excellent putting surfaces and with putters and balls far inferior to those of today, did amazingly well because of proper natural employment of the body in the stroking. Today's most consistent putters in major competition use more body than generally is recognized.

Lloyd Mangrum has been consistently one of the finest putters and chippers in tournament golf in recent years. This is due to his superb combination of hand and body action. He minimizes the risk of inaccuracy of line because he depends on shoulder action rather than on wrist action in stroking his putts for length. By maintaining his hands in the same relative position as in address he does not pull or push his putts off line. His putting style is a fine illustration of the basis of the American swing pattern—the hands for direction and the body for power. The foundation of this style is the same for the long drives as for the putts.

There is only one basic swing in golf.

It often astonishes the inexpert observer when the keen-eyed pro analyst points out identical routine performance in the swings of "Porky" Ed Oliver and "Bantam Ben"

Hogan. The fat man, the slim man, the big man, the little man—all swing the club the same way when they're swinging it correctly.

And there's no basic difference between the swings of competent women and competent men players.

Clubs to fit players

Difference in results obtained by players of varying physiques frequently is not due to the players themselves but to their clubs. American golf club design and construction are by far the best in the world and there is little excuse for a player having clubs that don't fit him in weight, length, lie, shaft whip, stiffness, or swinging weight.

When the professionals of the United States can make the golfing public realize the value of expert service in supplying clubs that fit the build and muscular condition of the player, they will have made tremendous progress to the players' advantage.

But, at this point, it must be noted that many a youngster developed a good golf swing because he started with a club or clubs discarded by some older person. This beginning equipment was unquestionably too heavy for the boy's hands to handle easily. Consequently the boy had to use a lot of body in his shots and subconsciously learned to be adept in footwork.

The adult student has lost, through athletic inactivity, his capacity for shifting his weight by correct footwork. That's why the first of the two basic lessons in American-plan golf associates footwork with proper hold of the club. Routines of the second lesson also involve footwork, simultaneously with hand action.

By these routines—and by them alone, as far as I have been able to discover—can the average golfer be relieved of bad habits acquired by thinking that power must come from strong hands and strong arms. It absolutely does not! Power in the golf shot comes from body action, and you can't have any better body action than you have footwork.

The most impressive demonstration of power in the golf shot coming from the body rather than from the hands is seen in the performances of one-armed golfers such as Jimmy Nichols, "Army" Gianvito, Vic Shipolia, and the late Louis Martucci. All of them hit wood and iron full shots the average length of good two-armed golfers.

For examples of inability of strong men and women to get distance in their golf shots, look at any of the thousands of muscular high-handicap golfers who make strenuous but incorrect use of their arms and bodies yet can't hit the ball 200 yards.

Frank Stranahan is one of the strongest men in golf. His weight-lifting training certainly has given him more powerful muscular qualifications for long hitting than anyone else who is prominent in the game. Yet he is not one of the long hitters.

Natural shifting of weight

The turn of the body and the shifting of weight in the proper golf swing is closely comparable to throwing a baseball, a full punch in boxing, kicking a football, a backhand stroke in tennis, a toss of a basketball, or the throw of a hammer. It is a perfectly natural action.

An illustration of this fundamental importance of weight shifting has been supplied by Sam Byrd, who succeeded Babe Ruth in the Yankee outfield and who later became a professional golf headliner. Sam had watched Joe Louis hit some golf shots on a practice tee. Joe came from practice wondering why, although he hit the ball so hard, it went only a moderate distance.

Byrd explained to him: "Joe, if you'd hit at other fighters with the weak footwork you have in golf, and they'd hit back at you with their weight shifted on their feet as a good golfer shifts his weight, you'd never have been heavyweight champion. You'd have been the one who was knocked out."

Footwork begins with the stance. By my own observation and that of hundreds of other professionals whom I regard as excellent instructors, there isn't one player in an average group of ten who realizes the importance of shifting weight properly, who understands how and why to shift his weight, or appreciates how correct weight-shifting depends on correct foot position or stance. They never get themselves set to hit a ball in the right manner.

If the stance isn't correct the player will find it impossible to shift his weight properly. Without the correct shifting of weight nobody can hit a golf ball well.

With superb footwork Hogan hit a ball about as far as those much heavier stars, Snead, Harbert, or Demaret. Louise Suggs and Patty Berg, when their normally excellent footwork is functioning so their bodies come into the shots perfectly, are not far behind the drives of "Babe" Zaharias with her magnificent strength and grace.

Hand "power" not essential

The old idea that it is necessary to have superbly strong hands to play good golf has been exaggerated. Lloyd Mangrum, for instance, says his wife has stronger hands and forearms than he has. That discovery will be made by almost any man who watches his wife take a spoon and whip a thick batter in a crock, vigorously for minutes; then tries the job himself and finds that it very soon tires him.

Willie Kidd is a veteran Scotch-born instructor whose keen observation and persistent research has contributed much to development of the American plan of instruction and play. Willie has pointed out that Harry Vardon, with large and powerful hands, made use of the "Vardon" grip to make positioning of the club more accurate and keep his hands "balanced" rather than to power the shot.

Tommy Armour and Bob MacDonald have two of the finest, biggest, strongest sets of hands ever seen in American golf. Any competent observer who has studied Armour's hand action for years, either in watching him play or in pictures, is completely convinced that a great element of Armour's artistry has been that of hand work for precisely positioning the club at impact rather than as a source of power.

MacDonald, some years back, gave a convincing demonstration of the fact that the hands need only hold the club firm enough to keep it in correct position while power is being transmitted from the body. Bob then was blasting a prevailing delusion that what makes golf difficult was that it is "really a left-handed game for right-handed players." He had an artificial left arm made and attached to his left shoulder and the club. He held the club with his right hand in his usual manner. With his own left arm hanging limply at his side MacDonald hit shots with power and precision.

During the past ten years, understanding of the source of power and its transmission and control has become clearer to professionals as we have been studying the "mechanics" of the golfer.

Difficulty of hand-action analysis

Our study of motion pictures has begun to yield results. We've been at that phase of study a long time but only comparatively lately have we appreciated that while the camera shows us the motions it doesn't separate the elements of the movements. For example, the left hand, being almost concealed from the camera, is difficult to study. Only by close examination and measurement was I able to confirm that a pick-up of the club by the right hand has a compensating thrust downward of the left hand by a slight straightening of the left elbow, in the very early stage of the backswing.

Despite the customary admonitions to drag the club back and keep the left arm straight, thousands of inspections of expert players, in person and in motion pictures, gave irrefutable evidence that the American method is contrary to what many of us have thought to be the common procedure of the stars.

There is another bromidic expression that has been proved to be a fallacy by study of players in person and in pictures. That is the recommendation to slow down the backswing as a cure for a fault or faults. As a matter of fact the backswing is fast if the player's temperament dictates. Bob Jones and Ed Dudley had rather slow backswings because the rhythm was in keeping with their temperaments. They swung back slowly and far and picked up a lot of speed when they came down through the ball. Snead's backswing is slow and far, too, but some excellent players who don't have full backswings swing rather fast (but without jerkiness).

The reason for a slow backswing is to permit employment of every essential detail of the routine. The routine must be coordinated in the same manner as operation of the clutch and gear-shift must be coordinated in driving an automobile. The backswing is too fast only when one of the necessary details has been omitted.

Studying swing pictures

Motion picture study sometimes is misleading to the professional as well as to the less experienced student because of improper location of the camera. When the lens is directly opposite the middle of the player then the picture is a true one of the front of the swing.

In American golf normal shots from good even lies are

played by the experts with the ball in a line extending out from the left heel or very slightly back of it. The reason they do this is that when the players are hitting, their weight is on the left foot and the ball in this position is in the logical location for receiving the hit.

Much has been contributed to the American plan of golf instruction by studying players from their right side. From such study, footwork, knee action, body turn, and positioning of the club frequently can be seen and understood more clearly than from a facing position.

I cite Bob MacDonald again as a notable pioneer in the American plan of play and instruction. Bob has called attention to the clarity with which balance and compactness of the correct swing can be observed from off the player's right side, in line with the intended direction of the shot. He reminds us that when wheels of a car are out of line the deviation can't be seen by looking at the broadside of the car, but only by standing in back or in front.

Tournament stars have contributed a great deal to the development of golf instruction in their diagnosis of each other and their own research. Their physical sensitivity, their frequent playing and practice and, in most cases, their backgrounds as golf instructors, enable them to respond to suggestions from companion professionals or to rectify their own faults or find some refinement of the fundamentals they can apply to their own games.

Difference between Diagnosis and Doing

Even with those advantages, it is surprising to see the difference between what these experts think they do and so state in their written and spoken remarks, and what they actually do in play. Consequently it isn't astonishing that the average golfer in trying to do what he's been told to do really does something at variance with instructions. The truth is that much of the average golfer's practice is worse than wasted time. He—or she—frequently is merely working to more firmly establish a fault.

Practice, whenever possible, should be under professional supervision. In many instances I've seen that the professional has determined what the pupil should practice. The lesson is explained to the pupil and to the pro's assistant if he supervises the practice. This is not only very helpful to the pupil but it also develops the assistant who has the one assignment of correcting a major fault. Hence the assistant is not disposed to bewilder the student with too much advice about too many details.

I know from experience with many hundreds of students that my summarized American plan, involving only four details in taking position and four in making the swing, comes quite close to making practice effective for the average golfer who is without expert supervision.

The pupil may need professional checking to see that the grip is as I describe it in the reading matter and illustrations later in this book. Or it could be that some malformation of the student's hands require that a competent professional alter the grip to suit the circumstances.

Then, too, the slight lift of the right hand with the accompanying downward thrust of the left hand at the start of the backswing may call for expert supervision before it becomes spontaneous with the student. A strange thing about this detail is that the right thing is done easily and naturally on a horizontal plane when an American boy starts swinging a baseball bat, but when the same boy grows up and becomes exposed to the technicalities of golf instruction he unnecessarily complicates this hand action.

I have my own troubles with some pupils in establishing the habit of correct hand action at this critical point. They have heard and read so much about dragging the club back with the left hand that it is difficult for them to make the right hand the controlling factor in this detail of the swing. I have them practice this stage of the routine first with the right hand alone and they do it correctly. Then I have them practice with the left hand alone and they do that correctly. Only practice can make perfect this necessary functioning of the hands.

Temperamental gaps in teaching

As long as golf instruction is concerned with the individual it can't be made completely mechanical or coldly scientific. There are bound to be temperamental gaps between the teacher and student in golf just as there are in other studies. Some of us as children had difficulty learning the fundamentals of arithmetic from one teacher, but learned them quickly and soundly from another teacher who taught by the same plan the first one used.

A confusing element in golf instruction is that not enough good instructors have the same plan of instruction. Some critics of golf teaching make the unwarranted allegation that there are as many plans of golf instruction as there are professionals. As a matter of fact there has been great progress made by professionals working through the Professional Golfers' Association of America to simplify, clarify, and organize instruction.

This advance in finding what to teach and how to teach it does not sacrifice the exceptionally high standard of individualism established by pioneer teachers of American golfers such as Alex Smith and Peter Hay. They and other Scottish and English professionals who came to the United States and taught successfully adapted the golf swing to the baseball batting type of swing that was natural to most Americans. The great effectiveness of these pioneers was in preserving these natural hand and body actions. They didn't get abstruse or go into a lot of details.

They simplified the task for their pupils by getting them to shoot golf as Annie Oakley shot a gun, according to the musical comedy song, by "doing what comes naturally."

American professional golfers have made a success of fitting golf to typical American temperament in class lessons for juniors. Junior golfers' averages today are at least 5 strokes lower than when the boys picked up their golf as caddies and without formal instruction.

Do it for fun—naturally

One thing professionals repeatedly have observed in teaching classes of boys and girls is that the mere fact that golf, a game, is being *taught* causes some of them to go at it awkwardly. These youngsters subconsciously believe that anything done for fun should be done in a natural way.

They're right, too. Outstanding coaches in every sport see some talented prospect who is getting results in a way that is natural to him but which may appear to have major differences from the prevailing style. By maintaining the fundamentals while developing any unique actions that are natural to the athlete these coaches make their students stars.

There may be some abnormal physical feature of the star athlete, who develops a style that is forced upon others it doesn't fit. The Bobby Jones straight left arm in golf is an example. Left hand control in positioning the club does not require the tenseness or straightness of the left arm that was a conspicuous feature of Bobby Jones' style. Present day star golfers rarely keep the left arm straight. They do have it comfortably extended but there is no appearance of rigidity or stiffness. During the Jones era Walter Hagen and Billy Burke were two whose left arms were obviously not straight but the Jones straight left was so distinctive most golfers tried to imitate that detail.

The golf professional has to spend much time and thought determining what are fundamentals and separating them from details of style peculiar to a golfer who happens to be winning frequently, hence is considered to be the model for all.

Golf instruction has improved generally as it has extended from the artist to become also the study of scientists. In this respect it has progressed along the same lines as other American sports. The art of the pole vaulter, hurdler, long distance runner, baseball player, or other athlete who has achieved outstanding success by procedures that are distinctive in him, eventually establishes standard style which is taught as such. Then along comes some greater performer with noticeable departures from the currently standard style. As a result of his performance other changes are made in establishing a new standard of form.

The experienced and qualified golf instructors know this story of progress. They study details of the experts' swings with as great—and possibly greater—thoroughness than the performances of stars in any other field of sport are studied by instructors. The nation-wide tournament schedule, the migration of professionals to the south and southwest in the winter, and the intimacy of play and locker-room talks give the golf professional better close-ups for study and analysis than are available in any other sport.

Basis of Learning

The professional, through years of study and trial and error, has a keen eye for details of the expert players' methods. The typical golfer hasn't the slightest idea of how to watch the stars in action so he can help himself better understand and use whatever professional instruction he receives. He doesn't put two and two together when he wonders why he hits a daisy or a dandelion easily and precisely but fails miserably when he tries to swing at a golf ball. At the little flower he's swinging naturally; at the ball he isn't.

And regardless of whatever the most proficient golfers may believe or say, their methods are the most natural to them, even though in some cases the naturalness was achieved after struggles in discarding unnatural and superfluous actions.

The average golfer who is taught by my American plan with its eight simple routine procedures learns what to look for in the performances of the experts and to understand why and how they function as they do.

By *starting with the clear idea that there are only two primary objectives in golf—direction* and *distance,* and by recognizing as the primary target the ball, not a landing area in a fairway, green, or the cup, the pupil then needs only to establish a hitting routine that will bring the clubface precisely in contact with the required clubhead momentum.

Formula for force

In high school physics the golfer probably learned the formula that is the base of everything about the golf swing. That formula is the formula for force—mass times acceleration.

Mass is the clubhead. Acceleration (time rate of change of velocity) is the rate the clubhead acquires speed during the swing.

You can't have the club too heavy to control with precision and without strain and tightness that slow the speed of the swing.

You don't get speed of the mass unless your body is correctly balanced to provide a steady hub from which the clubhead is swung with centrifugal force.

Now I think you've got the basis for acquiring mastery of the simple system I've devised for making a good golf swing. This system ALWAYS produces good results. I haven't had one case of a pupil who applied the system failing to improve his or her game.

I have had some cases in which the pupils say the system doesn't work. Then I get them on the practice tee and find that they haven't been using the system. They could have made that correction for themselves. All they had to do was to make sure that the directions—the successive steps in the system—were followed. Many of my pupils are motion picture actors and actresses. They develop by my system very quickly because they are accustomed to doing what their directors tell them to do in making pictures. They know the story. The director instructs them how to act it.

From the preceding material you have learned the story of the golf swing. You understand why and how the golf swing is a natural and simple series of instinctively coordinated details. You now are well ahead of many who are playing at golf. They haven't a clear idea of the principles of the swing.

All there is to the golf swing is a combination of power and direction. In golf, as in any other sport, the primary source of the power is the body turn.

Golf power must be applied through a club, hence it is necessary to have directional control through the elements nature has designed for this purpose—the hands. The hands set the club into the desired position and should maintain it in that position throughout the swing.

Coordination by instinct

Coordination of body and hand action is fundamentally instinctive. The nervous impulses travel too swiftly for you to consciously combine several of them in harmonious relation. The best that the most adept golfers can do is to practice enough to make coordination of the delicate details and refinements of the swing habitual. But the ordinary coordination of body and hands required by good golf is spontaneous when one sets one's feet to allow and encourage proper and natural shifting of weight and body turn.

The three essentials in a good golf swing are:

Footwork or weight shifting;

Body turn or pivot, which supplies the power;

Hand action or club control through which the power, accurately guided, reaches the ball.

2

Formula for the Swing

THERE ARE ONLY TWO MAJOR SECTIONS IN THE ROUTINE that will make you a good steady golfer. The first part is taking position for the swing. The second is making the swing.

During many years of teaching, I have found—and so have other professionals—that a great deal of the high handicap player's difficulty is the result of a faulty grip.

Almost invariably the better players have the club properly held before they address the ball. The high-scoring player doesn't. He gets up to the ball and makes adjustments in his grip, thus giving himself another essential detail to think about instead of going through a practically automatic routine performance.

He usually has read plenty about having the V's of the thumbs pointing to his right shoulder and tries to remember how many knuckles of his left hand he should be able to see. Thus he is confused before he even begins to get set to take aim at the ball.

FOUR ROUTINE STEPS IN TAKING POSITION

There is a very easy and positive manner of taking the correct hold of a golf club.

STEP #1

When you walk up to the ball have the club in your left hand with the thumb down the leather on the side of the shaft opposite the intended direction of flight. The ball of the thumb should press on the leather grip about at the 10:30 o'clock location on the shaft's circumference. The illustrations show this thumb position clearly.

Then you simply wrap your fingers around the leather. The club falls naturally in the firm position where the fingers can maintain a secure but not tense hold. The shaft runs diagonally from the "cradle" of the forefinger to the heel of the hand. The thumb and the forefinger are close together.

Now place the club close behind the ball with your left hand.

That's all you have to do and remember about the first essential. Your right hand, which hangs naturally by your side, already is in the correct plane and you step into the second phase of taking position.

STEP #2

Now you ADJUST YOUR FEET, with the ball on a line extending out from your left heel. Your right foot is placed in a comfortable position so your feet are just about shoulder-width apart. Toes are pointing slightly outward. A little more than shoulder-width separation of the feet won't interfere with your foot and body action, but don't have the feet too wide apart.

Have the toes on a line parallel to the line of flight.

When you walked up to the ball your knees weren't stiff, nor are they when you address the ball. Your knees are bent slightly so you may seem to be sitting down a bit to the shot.

With your legs stiff you haven't a chance to get full and controlled body action and power into a shot.

When you have soled the club so it lies flat on the ground behind the ball and have kept your right hand hanging down comfortably close to your body, the two factors necessary in making a good shot already have been assured without any confusing thought.

First: You are the proper distance away from the ball. The angle of the shaft with the clubhead and the length of the shaft assure that.

Second: Your left hand is directly in front of, and close to, your left leg. That means that the shaft is inclined forward slightly from the clubhead to your left hand. Your left hand is over the ball. Just that one little factor works miracles for the average golfer who suffers from chronically topping the ball.

Again, without having to think about a lot of details you have provided yourself with a partial guarantee that you will hit down into the ball instead of having the common fault of trying to scoop it up.

Club designers have devoted many years and considerable genius to devising clubheads that send the ball in the required trajectory when the ball is hit at the lowest point in the arc of the swing. Let the clubhead do the work for which it is designed and you'll get the ball up according to the loft of the clubface. In the case of the iron clubs with faces laid back—or lofted—more than the straighter faced driver and brassie, few average players realize that the sole of the iron is beneath the ball when the ball is being hit accurately with the center of the clubface. That is the reason for divots sometimes being taken after the ball is hit, especially when the higher lofted irons are used.

STEP #3

You need a simple and natural combination of two factors to give assurance of correct hand and body action.

You relax your right knee and bring the right hand around to the club.

"Long Jim" Barnes, years ago, was the first one who attracted any attention to this action of the right knee in associating footwork, body action, and the grip. Then I thought that Barnes' action with his right knee was simply a mannerism but the more I studied Jim's sound style and the more I analyzed prominence of the right knee action in the routine of expert players taking their position, the clearer it became that this was a significant detail.

When the right knee is relaxed and the right hand is brought around to the club the shaft of the club lies in the channel at the juncture of the fingers and the palm. The V of the right thumb and forefinger points toward your right shoulder, as does the V of the left hand.

The side of the right thumb is on the 1:30 o'clock position on the shaft. The right hand grip pressure is mainly that of the thumb and first two fingers. Firm control of the club, without any sensation of tightness, comes from this correct use of the thumb and the first two fingers of the right hand. The sense of muscle position is clearly "telegraphed" to the subconsciousness by the touch sensitivity of thumb and forefinger.

The little finger of the right hand is placed on the top of the left hand's forefinger. The thumb of the left hand lies snugly in the valley between the heel of the right hand thumb and the right side of the palm—along the "life-line."

The overlapping grip keeps a good balance in power and control between the hands. It also makes it comfortable for the thumb and first two fingers of the left hand to keep control of the club throughout the swing. The left hand primarily controls the position of the clubface. The right hand's hold on the club must be such that it coordinates smoothly with the left hand's function in determining clubface position.

Much is said about keeping the left little finger tightly around the grip—especially at the top of the backswing. This advice is contrary to what most star golfers with normal hands do. The left little finger is curled comfortably but not tightly in keeping the shaft in position. It is not a factor in securing a strong grip.

You don't hit the ball at the top of the backswing. That's where you get set to hit the ball. Your clubface must be properly positioned but it must not be held so tightly that the grasp retards a swift, flowing motion. When you curl your little fingers tightly you feel a muscular tightening in your arms, which you don't want until it comes spontaneously at the instant of impact with the ball. Otherwise that tightening tends to freeze and slow down motion.

STEP #4

The final action in taking your position is to TURN THE RIGHT HEEL SLIGHTLY AWAY from the intended direction of ball flight, so your right foot is at a right angle to the direction line.

Your left foot is pointed slightly at an angle ahead of the ball. This foot position is an essential factor in assuring effective body action to the normally built golfer.

Hogan has this foot position ideally. Nelson's right foot at address is pointed slightly backward at about the same angle his left foot is pointed forward. But anyone who has studied Nelson in action many times and has carefully studied many motion pictures of him will see plainly that he makes a quick, subconscious adjustment of the right foot so it's at right angles to the line of the flight shortly before his upswing begins.

The basis of my system is to eliminate all unnecessary

motions and adjustments. Hence this routine fourth move in getting you set so proper footwork is made easy and natural.

The typical golfer can't ever hope to groove his swing if he makes any unnecessary motions during the course of his swing. The expert who is muscularly adept has a keen sense of muscle position. He practices and plays so much he makes adjustments habitually in order to bring the club into proper position and can indulge in a few extravagances of motion. Nevertheless, when the experts do discover that they've got in their routine anything that involves an unnecessary risk to balance, club control, and swinging speed, they work to eliminate any such element and attain the utmost economy in effective action.

The position you're in after these four essential acts— placing the club with the left hand, adjusting the feet with relation to the ball, relaxing the right knee to get the right hand, arm, hips, and shoulders in proper address position, and turning the right heel slightly back—gives you the right foundation for making an accurate and powerful swing. You probably won't realize it until the first four positioning actions are a fixed habit with you, but by learning how to get ready to swing you've eliminated a number of the troubles that affect the typical golfer. There aren't two of a hundred average golfers who have the habit of getting set properly to the ball in order to have any chance of making a correct swing.

Four Routine Steps in the Swing

STEP #1

Now that you are correctly set, ready for action, your first movement is apparently a paradox. You make a forward press to begin your backswing. Practically every golfer has noticed what seems to be merely a slight wriggle of the star players before they begin to take the club back; that motion is the *forward press*.

What you do as the first action in making the swing is to bend the right knee a bit more forward. This turns the hips, body, and shoulders very slightly toward the cup and the hands are moved an inch or two ahead of the ball. The clubhead remains on the ground back of the ball. The entire action amounts to rocking the club forward.

This action is to unfreeze you from any tendency you might have had to become stiff in the address position. It gets the muscles working smoothly and prepares you for spontaneously correct footwork and body action. It starts you without a jerk and makes it easy for you to transfer weight properly for your backswing. You become a "man in motion" instead of a stiff, self-conscious mortal perplexed about how to get swinging smoothly.

If you begin from a dead start to make your backswing you are ruining your chances of power and smoothness just as surely as you would if you were to try to throw a ball by holding it up and tossing it without any preliminary action backward from the direction in which you intend to throw the ball.

STEP #2

Next, without any conscious pause from the forward press, reverse the action, rock the club back and go into the REVERSE PRESS. This is the key move of the golf swing.

You simply rock the club shaft back to where the hands are an inch or so back of being in line with the ball. This action bends the left knee in slightly and shifts weight to the right foot. But it doesn't tend to make you, subconsciously, stiffen your right leg. You still are sitting down a little to the ball.

What has happened is that, without realizing it or having to think about the details, you have started the hips, body, and shoulders in the correct route for the backswing. You have balanced yourself on the right foot so a free natural pick-up of the club can be made. You haven't swayed back and away from the ball but have simply effected a transfer of weight to be slightly heavier on the right foot. Now you are in position to make the proper combination of hand action in setting the clubface correctly, together with a turn of the body which swings the club back and up.

STEP #3

The third step in this process of making the swing is something that is in positive contradiction to much that has been said and written in golf instruction for many years. This third step, which sets the club in position, is a pick-up action of the right hand with a simultaneous downward counteraction of the left hand. This action sets or cocks the club as the body turns and swings the club back and up from the ball. It begins as the clubhead is being moved by arm and body action back a few inches along the direction line.

So many thousands of golfers have been warned against "picking up the club" early in the backswing that they never do get their wrists cocked. They push the club back with a stiff, straight left arm until they are off balance and leaning away from the ball. Then they never can get into position to use the body and hands properly. This warning against picking up the club too early is contrary to what every professional and amateur expert does in the American plan of playing. They pick up the club correctly.

Part of the difficulty in determining what actually happens at this stage of the swing is that the left hand, the controlling element in setting the clubface position, is concealed. Yet, when one examines slow-motion pictures carefully and focuses attention on hand action, it will be seen there is a critical functioning of hands at this point. This hand action is associated so closely with the beginning of the body turn of the proficient player that it virtually escapes discovery.

In the very informative pictures of Bob Jones' swing taken at the rate of 1000 pictures a second in 1940, the comment Jones wrote for the Spalding Research Laboratory is: "The relation between the shaft of the club, hands and arms does not alter noticeably until the fifth picture of the series. Practically all of the movement to this point has been accomplished by the arms and trunk."

The fifth picture of the series shows the hands about even with the top of the right pocket, which is the position at which most have said the cocking of the wrists begins on the backswing. But on close inspection of these Jones action pictures—as on minute observation of slow-motion pictures of other stars—there is discovered a definite alteration in the position of the hands between the first picture and the second picture of the backswing series. The alteration occurs too fast for the eye to catch when you watch the player but you can see the change in prints of slow-motion pictures.

The right hand has lifted slightly and the left wrist has pushed down and is bent very slightly toward the hole. The top-ranking experts thus have a vital primary means of positioning the clubface so it will be kept in proper position—straight across the ball and the path of backswing and downswing, or open when a slice is desired, or closed when a hook is wanted.

What may have prevented earlier and distinct recognition of this functioning of the hands in positioning the clubface before the backswing gets well under way was that this hand action often occurs during the waggle of a

professional's swing. Especially was that the case among
the older stars. Only comparatively recently was the waggle identified as a move that might have great significance
instead of being just a mannerism. Johnny Revolta in his
teaching has been prominent among those who developed
that discovery.

Tommy Armour was the first great player of the modern era to emphasize this extremely important action as
an essential of control. Anyone who has ever seen Armour
play must recall his repeated positioning of the club forward and backward, over the ball. Armour did take a little more time in making the shot after walking up to the
ball, but probably not as much time as would be required
for a wilder player's round. Once, in a tournament at Los
Angeles, the committee asked Tommy if he wouldn't mind
omitting his club positioning routine, which the committee
considered only a tedious habit. He graciously obliged
and the next day, without that action, was all over the
course instead of being straight as he normally was. Armour not only was the master of iron accuracy, but was
the straightest as well as one of the longest wood players.

I never saw Sandy Herd play, but I've had some of the
professionals who played with him show me his famous
and lengthy club "waggling." Instead of being merely a
loosening-up of the wrists, it was definitely a position-
setting action. Herd unquestionably was the most accurate golfer of the older generation. His record of 19 holes-
in-one is far, far ahead of any other professional. And he
could hit a ball long, too.

In books and in magazine and newspaper articles top
pros often say that no wrist action occurs at all in the
backswing until the hands are almost up on a level with
the right hip. But that rarely is the case in their performance. The average golfer, in making use of the techniques
of the experts, must have wrist action in positioning the

club very early in the backswing. In learning, this slight cocking of the club can be done as a noticeably distinct stage of the backswing and as the first hand action of the backswing. Later this cocking or positioning of the club can be done simultaneously with the foot and body action of the swing just as the expert does it in play.

Among the thousands of pupils I have taught successfully, seldom have there been any of such acute sense of muscle position that I could expect them invariably to get correct clubface position at the top of the backswing and maintain it firmly through contact with the ball. When there is no visual check-up on the clubface position the problem of getting and keeping the clubface correctly across the line of the swing is too baffling for most typical golfers to master. But by having the club positioned early in the backswing the pupil subconsciously is impressed by the right position where he can see it. He retains that correct position throughout the swing.

The suggestion of a downward push by the left hand in this club positioning phase together with centrifugal pull of the clubhead takes care of all the left arm extension the player needs. How many average golfers have added to their confusion and strokes by trying to keep a "straight left arm" and get a stiff, powerless, and awkward left arm, no one will ever know. Countless thousands also have made accurate and powerful shots impossible by worrying about keeping the right elbow down and comfortably close to the side as it should be on the backswing. Correct action of the left arm and proper positioning of the right elbow follow naturally, and without requiring attention to distracting details, when this clubface positioning is done early by the method I have described and which is illustrated.

With the clubface set in position the UPSWING is simply a matter of turning the body to the right with the

arms working in comfortable coordination with the body.
Your feet control your body action; your clubface position
is primarily set by your hands. So all the body action there
is to the upswing is caused by a turn or pivot with your
weight supported mainly on the right foot. The outside
edge of the sole of your right foot is the base of the body-
turning action on the backswing. The body turns around
as the required distance of the shot dictates. Your left
shoulder drops naturally and keeps from cramping you
as your body turns.

Your professional will remind you that if you are seeking more distance you will have to improve your body
turn or pivot, and make your swing longer. But you must
be sure that you retain correct hand action in club positioning. Sometimes there is over-emphasis on hand action
when the loss of accuracy is due to faulty pivot producing
a distortion that twists the hands out of position. The
body turn will carry your arms back as far as they need
to go. Your left heel is lifted naturally as the upswing
progresses and the natural and correct action of the left
knee is to move straight out, instead of sideways toward
the right toe, a direction which is unnatural and awkward.

There's more weight on the right foot in the upswing
because of centrifugal force in turning the body and
swinging the club to your right. However, correct body
action in turning around from the ball is made possible
by continuing to keep the right knee unlocked and even
slightly bent. A straight, stiff right leg in the upswing
makes re-shifting of weight impossible.

Some players, by body turn and wrist bending beyond
the needs of an easily controlled swing, get the clubhead
far back and think the greater length of the upswing arc
will give them greater distance. They aren't basically
right in this belief. You were reminded, earlier in this
book, that what determines distance is the force accu-

rately applied to the ball. The formula of force that the physics textbooks give is "*mass times acceleration.*" You must get velocity into your swing. You can't do that if your downswing starts when you are so far back you are out of balance and don't have the club under control.

The top of the backswing is a critical position. There must be no jerkiness at this stage. Most of the great golfers have very slight pause at the top of the backswing. They get set to deliver the punch right from the farthest-back point of the swing. A vast difference between the ordinary golfer and the fine performer is that the ordinary golfer begins his downswing before his backswing is finished. He doesn't let himself get as far back as the desired length of his shot requires. In his unthinking haste to hit the ball he stops his backswing with a jerk, then the spontaneous reaction is a flip of the hands which uncocks the wrists too soon, ruins timing, and destroys power.

When you get to the top of the backswing and are in good firm balanced position from the ground up, wait an instant to feel that sound position—even if you have to consciously tell yourself "WAIT"—until the slight pause at the top of your backswing becomes an established good habit.

STEP #4

Now all you have to think about is the final, pay-off phase of the entire routine, THE SWING THROUGH. This is done by simply reversing the turn of body to the left. This starts from the ground up, with your left heel coming down to the ground and the inner edge of your right foot pushing as its part of the initial movements. The left side straightens up as the body turns. From a slightly bent "sitting down" position the left knee becomes straight as the hips and shoulders turn to the left. What all the actions in the downswing add up to is a transfer of the weight so it will be supported mainly on the left foot.

You will notice from the illustration that the left side is quite obviously doing its proper share of bringing the clubface into proper position at the impact. Correct shifting of weight and correct club positioning account for the downswing's being a naturally coordinated series of motions that you can disrupt only by conscious effort.

Because the left leg began straightening almost at the start of the downswing there has been a slide of the hips, body, and shoulders in the direction of intended ball flight, rather than a pronounced turn away from the ball as in the upswing when the weight was primarily on the right foot and the right knee was slightly bent. This coordination of feet, legs, and body has the shoulders practically parallel with the line of flight as the clubhead is being brought close to the ball.

Correct footwork, which comes easy when you start with a good balance at the top of the upswing, makes the downswing simply a reverse of the upswing: a slide forward of the body, then a turn to the left. The left foot's position at an angle to the direction line is primary assurance of proper weight shifting and body turn in the downswing. When the average player thinks about the downswing as a matter of getting the weight back mainly on the left foot, his hips slide and turn naturally. Instead of lunging and losing his balance and power he stays firm.

By making the weight shift the primary action in the downswing the player protects himself against the most common error in hand action in the downswing. That error is beginning hand action at the top of the backswing instead of waiting until the hands get into the striking zone and should be in a position so the wrists will straighten spontaneously and accelerate the speed of the clubhead. Though much is said about the golfer's speeding clubhead action by straightening the wrists and whipping the clubhead into the ball from a starting point about two-thirds down on the downswing path, this precise timing as a conscious action is impossible for most golfers. It has to occur naturally in coordination with body action. When the hand action is allowed to follow body action in naturally coordinated sequence the player hits through the ball. He swings the club instead of letting the club swing him.

And as his feet have handled his weight transfer correctly he has no tendency to look up. His head hasn't been jerked out of position. It remains in a vertical line as the hub-cap of the swing wheel. As the follow-through nears completion the head turns naturally, just as the body has turned in the swing.

All Essentials in Eight Steps

The four routine steps in taking the correct position of address and the four routine steps in the swing are ALL the essentials. There just aren't any more! These essentials as presented here are in order and so simple that the basic routine is readily acquired as a habit. A highly important element of the American plan of teaching is that it enables the player to check up on his grip, stance, and swing. Or to explain it even more simply: to check up on his hand and body performance.

But the bad habits that most typical golfers have in their hand and body action are often so deeply rooted they are hard to eradicate. What baffles all average golfers most of the time—and the stars quite often—is the difficulty of diagnosing and correcting their errors. This difficulty is made disastrous for the average golfer because he not only hasn't the slightest idea of what is actually causing his bad shots but frequently is further confused by the volunteered advice of others equally uninformed.

A bad shot is simply neglect of one of the eight routine steps in body and hand action. As four of these routine details are cared for while standing still, nothing could be easier than eliminating 50% of the chances of error that cause bad shots.

The average golfer starts in the game without having clear in his mind just what is necessary to hit the ball correctly. He doesn't understand the fundamentals of the process.

The principles are few:

FIRST—There is only one swing in golf. The clubs produce the different effects. The driver, the brassie, the spoon, and the No. 4 wood produce the "driving" effect with differing degrees of loft. The irons produce primarily the lofting effect, with varying degrees of distance. The putter produces the rolling effect.

A big swing produces a big shot—in distance and loft. The small swing produces the small shot.

SECOND—The good swing is the same for everybody. It is not a case of an individual swing for each golfer. The principles that govern getting the clubhead into precise contact with the ball at the desired clubhead speed and with firm (though not rigid) balance are the same for a big robust fellow, a long, lean, limber player, or a small woman golfer. The golfer must fulfill the requirements of the swing. There is only one swing in which the minimum of margin of error and the maximum effectiveness in transmitting power and control to the ball are combined.

Some golfers, as I have mentioned, are gifted with physical abnormalities that enable them to get a plus value into the elements of the normal swing. Nevertheless the correct swing is based on normal human muscle, bone, and nerve functions.

THIRD—The body turn, or pivot as it's often called, is the major source of power for all the shots while the hands regulate the club position, thereby determining the direction of the ball's travel. This combination of body and hands is just as essential on short approach shots as it is on the long shots.

The Eight Steps

The six following pages contain an analysis in outline form of the eight steps that constitute the Novak system of par golf.

THE FIRST HALF:

What	How
STEP #1 Place Club to Ball	Do this with left hand. Be sure club handle is tilted forward so that left hand is over a point ahead of the ball. Left hand on top of shaft—three knuckles in view of player. V pointing toward right shoulder.
STEP #2 Adjust Feet	Left foot opposite the ball. Toes on a line parallel to line of shot. Weight even on both feet.
STEP #3 Relax Right Knee to Complete Grip	In order to bring right hand to the club, right knee must be relaxed. This shifts weight over to left foot and brings hand to the club in natural manner so hand is squarely behind shaft in sort of "slapping" position. Right hand (now more under club than on top) is directly opposite left hand, so when one "pulls" the other hand pushes. Balance of club or grip confined solely to first two fingers and thumb of both hands. This permits free movement of club.
STEP #4 Turn Right Heel Out	This outward turn of right heel moves foot from normal position of having toe pointed slightly outward to that of having right foot at right angle to line of shot, or even slightly "pigeon toed."

TAKING POSITION

Purpose	Result

This gives feel and sense of aim with the club.

This confirms "aim" by aligning body properly.

This move is most important. It gives proper "feel" of club in hands and yet this can't be done without proper adjustment of weight and body position. In effect it brings body, weight and hands together in coordinated relation to the club.

This series of moves teaches player to automatically assume the proper position to make the stroke. It provides a coordination of foot, body, weight and hand position which properly balances or poises the player for the swing while at the same time player gets feel of direction and feel of the club. When the four moves are completed player is balanced on left foot.

This gives more secure right foot position which is essential because one must be steady on right foot at top of swing. This move also relaxes right hip position so that full free turn to right can be made on upswing.

THE SECOND HALF:

What	How

STEP #1
Rock the Club
Forward

As the player is ready to start the swing, right knee is slightly relaxed and weight is on left foot, but left knee is not straight or locked. To start, right knee is bent forward even more (this is one of two moves of knee action necessary to shift the weight). This move is so common with good golfers that it has acquired a name and it is known as *"the forward press."* This action swings or rocks the club handle forward.

STEP #2
Rock the Club Back

After the forward press of the right knee is made, it is possible to change or reverse the knee position and, as the knees change position [right knee straightens (but not to a point of locking) and left knee relaxes and bends forward], the weight changes or shifts to the right foot. This, of course, is necessary so that player can turn body and swing club to the right. Club head remains on ground but hands and club handle rock over to the right and at conclusion of the move, hands are almost opposite right knee.

THE SWING
Why

As position is taken to the ball, player will find his weight shifted to the left foot, as it should be. However, player wants to swing or carry club to the right. This is impossible while weight is on the left foot, so a change of knee position must be made whereby weight is transferred to the right foot. This is the first of two moves in knee action necessary to shift the weight from left foot to the right foot.

If a person is standing erect with feet close together, weight will be evenly divided on both feet. When one knee is relaxed or bent forward, weight automatically goes to the opposite foot. This process of relaxing one knee and straightening the other is the natural way to shift the weight from one foot to the other and back and forth as desired.

Warning: Do not exaggerate this knee action, as weight then goes to wrong foot. This is why good golfers work their knees in such a modified way that the uninformed are not aware of the knee action.

Caution: While hands rock forward on step 1 and backward on step 2, be sure that feet remain on the ground on these two moves. On step 3 left heel is raised and on step 4 right heel is raised; but keep heels on ground during steps 1 and 2.

THE SECOND HALF:
(*Continued*)

What	*How*

STEP #3
Start Club with the
Right Hand

As the preceding move is completed, hands are rocked over to the right and at this point the club is really thrown into control of right hand. Only way to get the club into motion is to make a sharp, abrupt pick-up action with right arm. This pick-up action will develop a countering downward thrust on part of left hand. The downward thrust of left hand positions or cocks the club as desired. The hands, with the pick-up action of the right and the downward thrust of the left, actually immobilize each other so that the only recourse the player now has is that of turning the body to the right and thereby swinging the club up and away with a body turn or pivot.

STEP #4
Swing Through

As weight was shifted to right foot and right hand initiated the movement on the club that induced countering or downward thrust action in left hand, so the hands nullified each other against any further movement. Only thing player can do is to turn body to right. Now that top of backswing has been reached, only thing player can do is reshift weight to left foot and swing club through with a reverse turn of the body.

THE SWING
(Continued)
Why

Hands and body work together to swing the club up and away from the ball. The action originates in the right arm, develops counterwise in the left hand and arm which actions position the arms perfectly— the right one relaxed and close to the right side of body and the left one now becoming naturally but comfortably straight. In this position of natural opposition wherein neither arm can move, the only alternative is to set up a turn of the body to the right.

[Club is positioned or cocked with the hands so that direction and character of shot are thereby determined. This further forces player to use body turn to swing club back and forth, which is the natural way to swing the club. (All done in a natural sequence, yet almost simultaneously.) Can be practised separately and eventually done together.]

As explained under "how," only thing player can do is to reshift weight to left foot and swing club down and through with a reverse turn of the body. This motion is centrifugal action whereby one truly swings from the "inside out," in a full free "follow through."

3

Putting and Short Approach Shots

To ACHIEVE THE FINAL OBJECTIVE OF GETTING THE BALL into the cup, the same two requirements that are present in every other golf shot—direction and distance—are also basic requirements in putting. In putting the golfer must not only gauge the speed or distance of the putt but must also control the direction with finer precision than in the long shots.

A good golf swing in putts, as in the longer shots, is a matter of organizing oneself into a rhythmic continuity of motion wherein the body turn or pivot supplies the power while the hands impart this power to the club. This formula, whereby the player gauges his power or distance by the extent of his body turn, and controls the direction of the shot by setting or cocking the club in the desired position, will work on the putting green just as it works on the long drives.

Much of the bewilderment about putting is caused by failure to apply some elementary reasoning: "If it works on the long shots it ought to work on the short ones, or vice versa." The putting stroke is fundamentally no different from any other stroke in golf except that it is done on the most delicate scale—and when you have a downhill putt on a fast green you know what I mean.

50

Body in Putting

The idea of body motion in putting may at first sound rather startling but that great master, Bob Jones, subscribed to the idea and no one can deny that Jones was highly efficient on the putting greens. In Bob's own words he described putting: "First get a comfortable position with feet close together then sweep the club away from the ball, keeping the club low on the backswing. Follow through the same way. If there is any feeling of movement in the body let it move!"

I would like to have had Bob recommend controlling the putting stroke power with a body movement which of course is a true pendulum movement.

Another great player who definitely employed this body control in putting was Leo Diegel. So pathetic were Leo's efforts on three- and four-foot putts that he discovered in experiments that by locking first his right arm against any movement at all, and then his left arm, and eventually both of them, his putting improved. With this locked arm position Leo had to use his body to swing the club back and forth and he correspondingly kept the putter in a set position throughout the stroke so his putts were very accurate.

Take also into consideration the young caddies or other youngsters who practically swing and sway all over the green in a carefree way, yet roll the ball into the cup with uncanny accuracy.

Putting Routine the Same

So the logical and effective plan in putting is to adopt the same routine that has been suggested on the drives and the irons.

Take your position at the ball with the same four moves:
(1) Place the club closely behind the ball with the left hand;

(2) Adjust the feet, left foot opposite the ball, toes on a line. Keep heels very close together;

(3) Relax right knee to bring the right hand to the club but when the right hand comes to the club overlap with two fingers instead of only one. This will develop a more delicate feel and control in the hands;

(4) Turn the right heel out.

Now for the swing:

(1) A slight forward press;

(2) A reverse press;

(3) Start club with right hand. This will automatically develop an opposing downward action on part of the left hand (this downward thrust is felt and applied principally with the left thumb). This action of the hands kicks or lifts the clubhead off the ground slightly. At this point the body takes control and sweeps the club back and forth in a perfect pendulum movement while the hands keep the club steady.

The club is swung from the shoulders instead of being powered by wrist action. Notice how the consistently good putters among the tournament stars keep the wrists out of the putts, except for positioning the club, and you'll see how the principles of power and direction control I have set forth apply effectively in putting just as in the longer shots. And you also will see that most of the short putts—from four feet and less—are missed by depending on the wrist action rather than body action after the wrists correctly position the club.

Another thing you'll find by experience is that using body action for the "touch" or power of the putt minimizes the ruinous element of nervous "yips" when there is a particularly important and delicate putt to be made.

The first four pictures show how to take the proper grip, stance and general body position in four easy, natural moves.

Left arm in naturally easy position.

Three knuckles of left hand visible to player.

Note left hand is on top of club.

V of thumb and forefinger points to right shoulder.

Position of left thumb at 10:30 on shaft. Notice shaft is tilted forward so hand is over ball, not over clubhead.

Note that line between left heel and ball is at right angle to line of shot.

Toes on a line parallel to line of shot.

Feet about shoulder width apart.

V of right hand points to right shoulder.

Right hand is brought into position on club.

Right knee is relaxed.

Position of right thumb at 1:30.

Left toe pointing out in normal position.

Right heel is swung out so right foot is at right angle to line of flight. This gives firmness at top of swing.

SUMMARY: Player is now ready to start the swing. Ball is opposite left heel. Weight is on left foot. Hands opposed to each other on club. Toes on a line.

The pictures on this page and on the following page show the proper method of placing one's hands on the club.

Left thumb at 10:30 position on shaft. V of thumb and forefinger pointing to right shoulder. Three knuckles of left hand visible to player.

Note left thumb at 10:30 position and how leather grip runs diagonally from cradle of forefinger across palm. The club is held by the thumb and first two fingers.

BRINGING RIGHT HAND TO CLUB

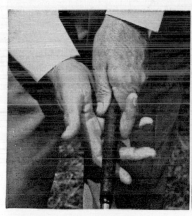
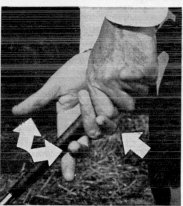

Little finger will ride *on top* of left forefinger. Club lies in the fingers of right hand, not diagonally across fingers and palm. Left thumb in center of right palm.

Little finger of right hand rides left forefinger. The thumb and first two fingers apply the pressure in the right-hand grip.

Little finger rides on top of (overlaps) the left fore-finger.

Hands are in opposing positions—when one "pulls" the other "pushes," and vice versa.

Hands are not tense.

With very few exceptions good golfers use this overlapping grip

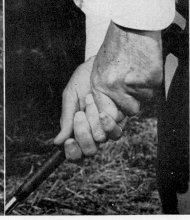

Right hand in correct hold and location for transmitting power and controlling the club.

Firm but not tense hold by thumb and first two fingers of right hand. Thumb and first two fingers of left hand are also the "holding elements."

PLAYING SPECIAL SHOTS

Much emphasis has been placed on the fact that the easy way to play golf is to "let the club do the work"—in other words, "use the same swing on all shots."

However, on the undulating terrain of the golf course there are numerous and varied positions in which the ball comes to rest. This is all a part of the game. There are no dull moments. There may be side-hill, down-hill, up-hill lies. The ball may land in a sand trap or in deep grass.

Again let me repeat, the player is still interested in "distance and direction," and the same fundamental requirements of the swing must be applied and adhered to, even though it may be rather awkward to perform because of the difficulty of the lie.

A slight adjustment of foot position and a slight adjustment of club position can in such cases work wonders, and here are some helpful hints.

Weight shift determines contact point in swing

Earlier in the book you were told that the experts all play the ball at a point approximately opposite the left heel. This is the proper thing to do in all normal shots, wood or iron.

Obviously, it is difficult if not practically impossible to move or swing the club away from the ball if the player keeps his weight on his left foot, and again if the player shifts his weight as required to the right foot for the backswing, it is impossible to swing down or through if the weight remains on the right foot. The rule is, then, that while the player assumes a position to the ball wherein the weight is on the left foot, the first thing he must do before the backswing can be started is to shift the weight to the right foot—then in order to swing through, the weight must be again reshifted to the left foot so the club can be

brought down and through the ball in a full free movement.

Why ball is played opposite left heel

The player is therefore always balanced if his weight
is on his left foot as the ball is being hit. The natural place
then to have the ball is at a point directly opposite the
left heel and, as previously explained, *this is how direction
is "lined up" or how "aim is taken" for a shot.* The ball is
always opposite the left heel and the shot will fly at right
angles to this line.

When to play ball opposite the right foot

However, if the ball is lying in a cuppy lie, in a depression, in long grass or sunk or half-buried in sand, then the
above procedure of playing the ball opposite the left foot
would result in topping the ball.

In all of the above cases, the proper thing to do is to
place the club in an abnormal position. The club should
be placed so that the shaft is tilted forward and the club
is deliberately turned down on the ball.

This placement of the club creates the effect of playing
the ball at a point more nearly opposite the right heel—
in other words, the ball is played farther back with hands
in normal position at a point ahead of the ball. The swing
is then made as usual with all the weight shift, pivot, and
hand action to keep the club in line, and the net effect
is that the ball is contacted earlier in the swing. The clubhead contacts the ball and then continues on down to the
lowest part of the swing, taking out a divot or piece of
the turf after the ball is struck.

How to Regulate Divots

The farther back the club is played the deeper the club
digs and the larger the divot.

It becomes therefore simply a matter of determining how far back off center (how far back off the left foot) it is necessary to play the shot, and the thing that determines that is how bad the lie is. The deeper the depression, the deeper the grass, the more the ball is sunk in the sand, the farther back the ball must be played so that the club is automatically set to go down after the ball. The above information should prove invaluable in getting the player out of the bad lies.

(But on good lies on the fairway it is not necessary to play the ball back and many needless divots can be avoided.)

Chip shots

In addition to bad lies, the above procedure of playing the ball back off the left foot will prove invaluable on chip shots or all short shots around the green. By so placing the club to the ball, the clubhead will nip the turf ahead of the ball. This will also automatically create a nice pickup of the ball and definitely insure one against topping, which of course is bad at any time but fatal on the short approach shots.

Cure for topping the ball

While on the subject of topping, which incidentally is one of the commonest faults of beginners and high-handicap golfers, it can be explained that topping is generally caused by the failure of the player to shift his weight to the left foot soon enough in the downswing.

Special effort and practice must be concentrated on this phase because all of us are more or less right-handed and we are prone to stand and balance ourselves on our right foot most of the time, if not always.

However, by following the procedure suggested, the player will soon learn to slide over to the left foot; only in that way can proper contact be made with the ball. However, the most difficult thing for some high-handicap golfers to learn is that uniformly good results cannot be had in golf unless the player learns to hit or swing down onto the ball instead of trying to scoop it up.

If such topping is a consistent fault, the practice of playing the ball back will prove very helpful.

The push shot

The above procedure, which so easily gets a ball up and out of a bad lie, has been often referred to as a "push shot," a shot that is used to play low shots into a wind. It has been presented as something that only experts should attempt, when in reality it is a certain, sure way to get out of a tight spot, provided of course that the player is reasonably well grounded in the fundamentals of the swing, to wit: weight shift, pivot, and hand control of the club.

In all such shots it is best always to keep the face of the club slightly closed because of the emphasis that has to be put on following through so that the full effect of the club can be had on the ball.

Sand trap shots

Nine times out of ten, playing the ball back more opposite the right foot will automatically get the ball out of sand traps or bunkers. However, the player who finds his ball in the sand should determine two things from the way the ball lies and decide before he plays the shot just what to do about these factors.

The first consideration is just how the ball lies—does it lie on top of the sand or is it partially or totally buried?

The second consideration is to decide whether to play the club in the regular, closed position or whether circumstances necessitate the use of the open-face club position or a "cut shot" to produce a quick rising shot.

When necessary to get distance from the sand, play the ball clean because any sand between the club and the ball diminishes the impact on the ball. Taking a lot of sand or taking just a slight amount of sand is used by good players as a definite means of controlling the distance of trap shots around the green.

Quick-rising shots

While the ordinary trouble shot procedure, that of playing the ball back opposite the right heel, is recommended for trap or sand shots because this method will get the ball up and away and also give the player a chance to control the amount of sand taken on any shot, there are times in a trap or bunker when this type of shot will prove ineffectual because it does not raise or loft the ball quickly enough.

There may be a steep bank or sand wall which may stop such a low-flying shot. In such a case, the player should reverse the procedure and play the ball forward off the left foot. Also in this case the player should deliberately "open" the club at the outset of the backswing so it is possible to deliberately cut across the ball and lift it sharply with a slice action.

The shot which is known as a "cut" shot is very effective out of deep grass which is close to the green, although the regular procedure of a trouble shot, wherein the ball is played back opposite the right foot, will be found to be an easy and effective way of actually pulling or dragging a ball out of a deep grass lie which borders some greens. This procedure, using a niblick or sand wedge, will give a most delicate control when needed near the green. In fact, on all short *chip* shots, where a pitch and run effect is desired, the ball should be played as suggested in this trouble shot procedure, that is, opposite the right foot.

Hooks and slices

There are, in effect, only three kinds of shots in golf: high-flying shots which tend to break or curve off to the right, and when exaggerated, become slices; low-flying shots which tend to pull or draw to the left into hooks; the in-between shot, the straight shot, which as a rule is perfect in flight and trajectory, being neither too high nor too low.

No player can really feel that he has mastered the game of golf until these hooks and slices can be played at will. From the ability to hook or slice, by being able to play first one of these shots and then the other, the player can strike a happy medium and drive them straight. There is no great art or skill required in order to hook or slice. If a player is properly grounded and trained in the fundamentals of a golf swing so that he knows why and how to shift his weight, also knows why and how to use his body to swing the club through the pivot action, *then it is a simple matter "to rock and set the club" so that the corresponding hook or slice can and must be executed as desired.*

Whether the ball is to go high with a backspin or low with a "run," whether the ball is to slice off to the right or hook to the left, is something that can be definitely controlled and determined by knowing how to "set the club" before the body takes it off into the swing.

The rules that govern are these:

(1) If the club is cocked or set in an open position the law of physics, "The angle of reflection is equal to angle of incidence," will apply and the ball will turn off to the right.

(2) If the club position is reversed, i.e., closed, the ball will be met "from the inside" which of course will make it turn or fly to the left.

(3) If the club position is in between the above two, or square to the line of flight, then the ball will fly true and down the middle.

This principle of club position governing the flight of the ball is just as positive and elemental in golf as the positioning of the cue in the hands of a billiardist whereby he produces follow or reverse english on the cue ball.

If there is any phase of the golf swing that savors of sleight of hand artistry it is the part of the swing wherein the club is "positioned," "cocked," or "set," for the shot (these three terms are used interchangeably). And this so-called cocking of the club is the very essence of the shot.

Instinct vs system

Many fine golfers will wiggle and waggle the club, and purely from instinct maneuver the club to a position from which they can hook or slice at will, but it is my hope that the following outline will give you a definite plan to play your hooks and slices and from that learn to keep them down the middle all the time.

SLICES

In the slice the ball starts off to the left of the intended line of shot and then curves out to the right. This is a high flying shot which drops dead and, as a rule, has very little roll. It acts like a boomerang and if it were hit hard enough would almost curve to a point where it would start back to the player. A player who slices cannot get any distance on his shots because of this tendency of the ball to come back to him rather than to go forward and away from him. This is a common fault in golf.

Why slicing is common

The reason that slicing is such a general fault among golfers is that many golfers do not understand the importance and the necessity of shifting weight. Because they fail to shift their weight, they cannot pivot or use their body to swing the club. They are forced to start the club away from the ball with their hands and arms and the natural result is that they roll the club away from the ball with a pronating movement of the left arm which carries the club back to an open position—that is, the club face is rolled away or turned up toward the sky. Now unless the club is rolled back on the downswing (which of course would be one fault added to another) the club must be brought down across the ball with the club in an open position and a slice must occur.

Cause of shanking

No weight shift and no pivot, which produces a slice so readily, leads to another fault. Often as a player takes the club back with hands and arms only, there is a strong tendency for the weight to list to the left foot as the club is raised on the backswing. Weight on the left foot and club in an open position at the top of the swing almost invariably produces a "shank," the most sickening shot that befalls a golfer. In this shot the ball is hit with the heel or socket part of the club and it slides off to the right in an uncontrolled manner.

This "shanking" disease generally occurs in short approaches where the player is very apt to be hesitant to pivot.

How to slice

To deliberately and intentionally play a slice the procedure is as follows:

1. The ball should be played at a point slightly ahead of the left foot.
2. The club is placed so that the toe is turned in slightly and the shaft is perpendicular, not tilted forward.

From this position of the club the left hand is more or less in front of the shaft, not on top of it. The knuckles are not showing as suggested in the regular grip where three of the knuckles of the left hand are showing. This position also makes it more natural to put the right hand more on top of the shaft rather than under the shaft.

This emphasis on grip and club position is required, because the way a club is placed and gripped has a lot to do with how the club is going to be cocked or set for the shot in mind. In addition it is helpful also to assume a foot position or stance which lends itself to a slice or hook.

Stance for slice

In the slice shot it is best to bring the right foot slightly nearer to the imaginary line between the ball and the hole. This projected foot position places the body at an angle which makes it easier to bring the club across the ball as desired in a slice shot.

Now, after the club grip and stance have been taken as suggested above, a normal routine will automatically produce a slice.

The procedure is as follows:

1. Rock the club forward—this is done with a slight forward action of right knee.
2. Reverse the club position—that is, rock the club back. This is done by reversing the knee position which of course shifts the weight to the right foot. Then. . . .
3. Start the club from the ball with the right hand but as this is done be sure to let the left hand turn in toward the body sharply so that the club is cocked "open"—that is, tilted so that the face is turned away from the ball and the shaft of the club is thrown out away from the player to a point outside the line of the shot.

From this point with weight on the right foot and club cocked or set with "face open" and shaft outside the line of the shot, the body turn on the right foot carries the club up to the top of the swing. Then. . . .

4. A reverse shift of the weight to the left foot and reverse turn of the body pulls the club down and across the ball and a natural slice shot, that is, a curve of the ball to the right will occur.

PROCEDURE FOR HOOK

To hook the ball, that is, curve it to the left, the procedure is the same except that the club must be set or cocked in a closed position, that is, the clubface must be turned to the ground and the club shaft must be set on the inside of the line of the shot. The club is set in a position exactly the reverse or opposite of the slice position.

Whereas in a slice the clubface is open and the shaft pointed out or across the line of the shot to the outside, in a hook the club face is closed (turned toward the ground) and the shaft is pointed in toward the right toe so that it is on the inside of the line of the shot.

Stance for hook

For the slice the club was placed out forward, in front of the left heel. For the hook the club is placed back towards the right foot more like the position for a "trouble shot." The clubface is kept square with the ball and the shaft tilted forward as the club is placed to the ball.

The left hand, instead of being in front of the club handle with no knuckles showing, is now well on top of the shaft with fully three knuckles showing. The right hand is well under, not on top of the shaft.

The right foot is drawn back away from the ball so that the body is turned away from the intended line of shot and the shoulders are pointing to the right of the line of the shot.

The regular procedure is followed in the swing.

1. The first move is the forward press.
2. The next move is the reverse press wherein the club is rocked back, the position of the knees is reversed, and the weight is shifted to the right foot.
3. Now comes the move which is critical in all golf shots, the positioning of the club. For the hook, the club is started the same as it is in every shot in golf, with a sharp pick-up action of the right hand while simultaneously the left hand with a downward thrust positions the club. In this case of positioning for a hook the left hand rolls out and away (counter-clockwise) from the body (reverse of the slice action wherein left hand at this point rolls in toward the body) and the clubface is turned toward the ground. At the same time, the shaft is tilted in toward the right toe so that the club is set on the inside of the line of the shot.

   The turn of the body on the right foot brings the club up to the top of the swing, then. . . .
4. A reshift of the weight to the left foot is made so the body turn can be made on the left foot. This body turn swings the club down onto the ball. From the way the club was set the club swings out over the line of the shot and a natural hook or turn of the ball to the left takes place.

Side-Hill Lies

It has been emphasized, and properly so, that direction in a golf shot is determined entirely by the hands through the manner of positioning the club. Also, that distance or power is a direct result of body turn or pivot as it makes the club swing through the ball. This system or formula is correct and when positively applied will produce positive effects.

However, a faulty or negative effect of the hands will not only affect the direction but in turn influence or affect the distance. For example, if a player makes an otherwise perfect swing but through a faulty hand action permits the club to drop to an open position, then not only will the ball slice but it will fall short of the distance the ordinary shot would produce. The reverse effect would be true if the club were faultily closed.

In the same manner, a faulty action of the body not only affects distance but also affects direction. For example, if a player reaches the top of the swing perfectly, and then fails to shift the weight to the left foot, naturally a distorted action will occur in the downswing which would most likely turn or roll the club over into a hook motion. Likewise, an exaggerated slide to the left foot would make the club drag through and across the ball and thereby tend to produce at least a fade, if not a slice.

So it is then, that if a player finds the ball in a position where it is higher or lower than the level on which he is standing, a subsequent torque is produced in the body turn and consequent hooks and slices will occur.

Whenever the ball lies on ground higher than that on which the player is standing, the natural tendency is to hook or pull the ball to the left; when the ball is below the player the tendency is to slice. The best procedure to follow is to allow for the above results and deliberately aim to the left or the right as the case may require. That is to say, if an expected hook or slice would prove disastrous, that is, put the ball out of bounds or into a bad lie, then the player must and can compensate for it by deliberately "opening" or "closing" the club at the outset of the backswing in order to control the direction of the shot.

A helpful suggestion in the case of all side-hill, up-hill,

or down-hill lies is for the player to keep his knees more relaxed, bent so that freer movement can be had in both directions of the swing in the matter of weight shifting. If one does not shift weight both ways he is bound to lose balance and dub the shot. Don't take too big or too long a swing in these lies; use a stronger club wherever the situation permits. For instance: if the lie is good, instead of a full swing with a No. 7 iron use a one-half or three-quarter swing with a No. 5 iron.

Study the situation and be governed by whether the green can be reached in one shot—whether it is wise to try to reach it in one shot—or whether the desired score can be secured by playing surely and safely.

LEFT-HANDED GOLF

While this may not be the best place in the book for this chapter, nevertheless I do not feel that this book would be complete without some reference to left-handed golf.

There is no reason why left-handed golfers cannot play as well as or better than right-handed golfers. Golf is in effect a two-handed game, and a two-legged game. It has been explained that it is necessary to establish a working arrangement of both right and left hands in positioning the club and that both hands are necessary in order to keep the club in control throughout the swing; also it has been demonstrated that a golfer must shift his weight to the right foot for the upswing and back to the left foot for the downswing. So the player has to learn to use both feet and both sides of his body.

To play left-handed golf just reverse the 1-2-3-4 outline for position and the 1-2-3-4 outline for the swing. In my work at the University of California at Los Angeles, after the students thoroughly understand the form and the count,

I make them reverse the form and swing left-handed. This gives them a look at the swing from the other side and naturally gives them a better understanding.

Any good golfer can, when the occasion requires it, reverse his grip and play a good left-handed shot if the ball is up against a tree or fence which prevents a right-handed swing.

Just to prove this point let me relate an experience of many years ago. A friend of mine and I, dressed in street clothes, were strolling down the street while visiting in a distant town. Neither of us was recognized when we entered a golf school on the street level. I stepped up on the mat from which they drove the golf balls and using a right-handed mashie I assumed a left-handed position to the ball and began to make a motion to strike the ball with the back of the club.

By this time the person in charge came forward and said, "You can't play golf that way."

I said, "Why not?"

"Why, you are trying to play left-handed" was the answer.

"Yes, I understand that," I said, "but this club seems rather awkward; nevertheless this is the only way I'd like to play."

"Well, it can't be done," came the answer.

"Why do you say that?" I insisted.

"Well," answered the man, "golf courses are not built for left-handed players."

With that, I turned the club upside down so that the toe of it was pointed down to the mat, making it a left-hand club. Then I swung it up in a big swing and came down on the ball with a solid resounding smack. I dropped the club and we walked out, leaving the confused man to figure his own way out.

All of which proves that golf can be played both ways,

right- or left-handed, and in fact both ways with either right- or left-handed clubs. Try it.

Topping

The first fault generally suffered by beginners is topping. They're told they don't "keep the eye on the ball." They don't, but that's a result, rather than a cause.

Actually what is by far the most frequent cause of topping is lack of footwork and proper weight-shifting, which is the only way the proper body turn can be developed.

Check up on the position of the ball with relation to the feet. Make sure you get the forward and reverse "press" details of the swing routine and be sure to get back to the left foot on the downswing. That way you'll cure topping.

Hitting behind the ball

This is also usually the result of improper weight-shifting, especially failure to shift weight to the left foot at the start of the downswing.

Slicing

Clubface is in an open position. Often this is caused by a very tense grip with the left hand which forces the left wrist to turn in toward the body on the backswing. This rolls the clubface open so the clubface is drawn in and across the ball and a slice must occur. In gripping the club the left hand may be too far in front of the shaft and the right hand may be too much on top of the shaft.

Failure to shift weight to the right foot at the start of the backswing also produces this open position of the clubface, with a slice the result.

Hooking

This often is caused by failure to shift weight to the left foot at the start of the downswing. When the player keeps his weight on the right foot as the club comes forward on the downswing the club may turn over as it comes through and pull the ball off to the left in a smothered hook. By pausing for an instant at the top of the backswing you encourage the tendency to make a correct shift of weight subconsciously as the initial action of the downswing. That good habit (pausing at the top of swing) greatly reduces the hooking and slicing that results from improper transference of weight.

In curing the hook also check up on the grip. In hooking the right hand may be too far under the shaft and the left hand too much on top.

Shanking

Shanking is in reality an exaggerated slice.

A tense, tight grip with left hand and weight on *left* foot at the top of the swing will produce shanking (hitting the ball with the heel of the club).

Lack of pivot, a common fault on short approaches, also causes shanking.

4

Learning to Learn Good Golf

A MAJOR DIFFICULTY IN GOLF IS THAT THE PLAYERS DO not "warm up" as players do in baseball, football, basketball, tennis, and most other sports. Without any physical preliminaries, except possibly a few moments on a practice putting green that may not be of the same speed as other greens on the course, the player steps on the first tee and begins in a cold sweat of uncertainty.

Even the best and most experienced players feel shaky when they address the ball on the first tee of a tournament and have to drive it far and straight down a dangerously narrow lane between two rows of spectators. But, as you've probably noticed, the first drives of the better players are almost invariably exhibits of their finest type of performance. The explanation for this is simple. Generally their stage fright keeps them from thinking and they swing entirely by habit, unimpeded by any conscious attention to details.

At rare times, when an expert has been troubled by some fault in his grip, stance, or swing, he will be particularly careful about checking details before he makes his first shot. He has practiced and studied his fault and its correction and he will be sharply conscious of the necessity of having everything right. Consequently he gets off the first tee with a fine shot.

The typical golfer swings in paralyzed confusion and vague hope, not knowing which one of many faults may arise to plague him in the presence of others who are at the tee. He is up against the problem of giving himself a golf lesson quickly and sometimes he may not know where or how to begin. It never has been impressed upon him that his golf swing should have been systematized so he can go through the motions in a routine manner and with high confidence of success.

Rarely does the average golfer realize that his trouble is not as much the result of doing something wrong, as it is omission of some essential action.

For instance, because of failure to shift weight at the start of the backswing the player obviously must arrive at the top of the backswing with weight on his left foot. From such a position, about all he can do is to pound at the ball with his right hand. Any suggestion that he use his left hand would be futile. The player has put himself "out of business" by an error of omission rather than one of commission.

"Warm Up" Thinking

The golfer seldom realizes clearly that he must "warm up" his thinking for the game. Flourishing a club vigorously on the tee with the hope that he's limbering his muscles for a fine golf swing does him little, if any, good when he doesn't know how to use those muscles. A "warm up" for the purpose of keeping his head down, or his left arm straight, or his right elbow fairly close to his side in the backswing is usually completely futile. This is also true when it is done with the intention of suddenly making habitual any of the many things his volunteering friends have told him that he must do.

Some thought must precede making a golf swing routine. Actually, shifting gears in automobile driving requires coordination of about the same sort necessary to make a correct golf swing. The gear pedal must be pressed down, the hand lever shifted to its proper location, then the foot pedal released with about the same precision of timing one must employ when doing the footwork and handwork of golf correctly.

A Lesson Each Round

A lot of planning went into the organization of the American style of golf play. You hear some very good players say they never had a golf lesson in their lives. Every time I've heard that said by a proficient golfer I know that the one who makes the statement has been getting a fine golf lesson each time he or she plays because that golfer has been thinking the lesson.

Take the case of Sammy Snead as an example. Sam was an excellent athlete in high school in the West Virginia hills. When he started golf after being exposed to the game as a caddy, he began with a crosshand grip. An older brother slapped him out of that, so Sam tells. That was the only golf lesson deliberately given Snead. Simply by the actions natural to sports Sammy became a fair golfer quickly but he had trouble getting a ball up into the air. He had to drive with a spoon. You can readily imagine that his trouble must have been serious because, with Snead's naturally fine footwork and body action, a slightly closed clubface would be more of an asset than a fault.

Then he gave himself a lesson that many still have to learn. He placed the club on the ground behind the ball as it should be when the ball is being hit. With that grip at address he lifted the club in front of him, then he cocked his wrists so the club came back over his head.

After that he turned his shoulders and body so they'd be as they should be at the top of the backswing. Then, by studying the position of his wrists and hands at this point, he discovered that he'd been turning his wrists and closing the clubface at the top of the swing. When he'd given himself this lesson and determined the correct hand action, Snead was on his way to becoming a champion.

Snead's marvelous timing and physique gave him the foundation for extraordinary talent as a golfer, nevertheless the lessons he thought for himself and the putting lessons thought out with the help of Victor East and Vic Ghezzi were essential to his development. He maintains that he plays best when he isn't thinking; that his thinking must be done well ahead of each shot.

Organize shot-making thought

Almost every ordinary golfer will be reminded of a mental attitude somewhat similar to Snead's when he recalls that, after having played a bad shot, he dropped a practice ball and thought in advance of doing some simple little thing. This little thing—perhaps having the feet in the right position relative to the ball—meant having the second shot (the shot that was thought in advance) come off in a highly satisfactory manner.

Organizing your thinking is the first move toward good golf. It doesn't occur to us that a stupendous advance in thinking was made by the dawn man who first discovered that a pebble could be moved by hitting it with a club instead of by having to stoop, seize the ball in a hand and toss it forward. Yet many golfers revert to primitive type in failing to think of the club as an extension of the arms.

Organized thinking explains the achievements of every great golfer. But, because the subject happens to be golf instead of commerce, surgery, law, medicine, or literature, thinking is usually not considered a very important factor.

Armour and Hogan

As examples of people who use sound thinking in golf, Tommy Armour and Ben Hogan stand out in my mind. Armour was a first-class amateur in Scotland before he suffered the combat damage that kept him battered and under the threat of blindness in an army hospital for many months. During that time he thought out the golf game that not only made him an expert player, but one of the prominent influences on modern golf instruction.

Armour's closed stance was his solution of the problem of keeping the clubface square to the line on the backswing, hence giving greater assurance that it would be square at the instant of impact. Others, especially Nelson, developed more upright swings with this same objective of minimizing the risk of the clubface getting off line. Of course, hand action was a primary and associated element in all efforts to think out the manner of keeping the clubface precisely under control.

Hogan, when he was in the Army Air Force, gave himself a lesson by studying some action photographs of his swing taken while testing a slow-motion movie camera. Although Hogan didn't have opportunity to play, except during widely separated week ends, his study of these pictures gave him the foundation for much greater consistency and precision after the war than he'd had before going into uniform.

A most valuable element of my method of instruction is that it helps the player organize his thinking as well as his swing. Like other professionals, I found that to get the pupil in a frame of mind conducive to learning was just as important as it was for the pro to have a sound knowledge of the golf swing.

Basic Understanding of Actions

To get into the mood to learn the pupil must understand clearly the basic reasons for each of the few fundamental actions. This is frequently difficult for the adult golfer because he has read or heard so much about details of the swing and never has had his confusion cleared by simple explanations of the reasons for these actions.

For instance, so much has been said about the left arm being straight and the left hand having a firm hold of the club that the commonest fault of the high-handicap player became that of not using the right hand enough. It hadn't been made clear to the player that balance of the hands and smooth counter-action of the right and left hands are essential to keeping the clubface position controlled and transmitting body power with maximum effectiveness.

The reason for the Vardon, or overlapping grip, is that it sets the hands so that it is almost automatic for them to counterbalance properly. There is a natural tendency for the left hand to have control of the clubface position and the right hand to function as the primary coupling between the body, or the source of power, and the club. Coordination of these two "musts" is most generally and easily achieved by the overlapping grip.

Abnormalities in the fingers and palm structure of some players or bad gripping habits that require drastic alterations from normal may dictate departures from the overlapping grip but such cases are quite rare.

Macdonald Smith's Method

One of the men who exhibited one of the best methods of holding the golf club properly was the late Macdonald Smith. "Mac," as may be remembered, was uncannily precise in his play. That, of course, is a certain sign of correct handwork.

"Mac" walked up to the ball with the club held naturally in his right hand. He placed the club behind the ball with the right hand, then took his stance. After that he placed his left hand on the club in a free, but not tight fit with the right hand. He used the overlapping grip.

Some may wonder why I cite Macdonald Smith's approach to the ball and the grip inasmuch as the first step in my system is to place the club behind the ball with the left hand. There are several reasons. One is that I have found that the typical golfer is subconsciously made to pay more attention to the proper position of the ball in relation to the position of his feet if the left hand initiates the routine. Another reason is that it establishes the habit of correct grip by demanding a bit of conscious mental effort by the player. I want the pupil to get the habit of using his mind in getting set for a golf shot. Macdonald Smith thought out the right-hand approach for himself. In the cases of golfers who don't play as much as Mac did, the tendency is to have the right hand too far under or over the shaft of the club.

Still another reason for the first routine in my system (the left-hand placing of the club) is that it is unnatural for right-handed people to concentrate, subconsciously, on getting evenly balanced on both feet. After careful observation of hundreds of students years ago, I found that the right-hand approach, in the "Mac" Smith manner, developed an inclination to favor the right foot and encourage a sway instead of a swing away from the ball.

CHECKING ON THE SWING

In checking a golf swing there are three things that must be considered.

The first thing to watch is the footwork.

The next thing is the body turn or pivot; but, since footwork and body turn are so closely associated as to be in effect equal factors as indicators of merit or fault, a checkup on the footwork is usually adequate to determine whether or not the pupil is getting the proper body position to apply power to the shot.

The third and last thing to check is the action of the hands, whereby the power which the body turn generates is transmitted to the club.

This three-point system of analyzing the golf swing has been used with success in rating the form and shot-making consistency of experts prior to their tournament performances. With such a checkup it has been possible to determine those who are on or off form, where and why they are on or off form, and to make rather accurate predictions as to the winners.

FOOTWORK

There has been a distinct change in footwork in championship golf during the past 20 years. It was Alex Morrison who first gave prominence to this alteration when, in his teaching and in his first book, he made much of a roll on the insides of the soles of the feet instead of the marked rise of the left heel and twist of the left foot in the backswing which was a feature of the footwork of the older men and women stars.

There was considerable controversy about Morrison's emphasis on this significant detail. Among the younger players at that time, Henry Picard and Horton Smith in particular gave considerable attention to this modernization of footwork. What it amounted to was noting the importance of a detail that had been regarded merely as a mannerism of some powerful and precise players but which actually was fundamental form in providing a firm base for shifting balance in the simplest way.

Differences between mannerisms, form

Horton Smith and Henry Picard always have been "thoughtful" golfers. One of the first things they learned about golf was *how to learn.* Their style had considerable influence on younger players who had the imitative capacity. I recall that when Horton was playing very well his left knee dipped toward the ball more than was the case with most of the older good players. Some consider this detail a mannerism rather than an indication of fine footwork.

The distinction between individual mannerisms and details of basic good form often is confusing to the student. I know that when I was learning to play and later, when I was learning to teach, I frequently noted mannerisms that I thought were part of the "secret" of fine players. Later I discovered that they were only superfluous motions peculiar to individuals. But other actions that I thought were simply showy habits actually were revelations of some highly important detail of address, weight shifting, body turn, or hand action.

I have mentioned among these strongly significant actions the turning in of Jim Barnes' right knee at address, Macdonald Smith's placing of the club behind the ball with his right hand and Tommy Armour's lengthy waggle and manner of placing the club in front of and behind the ball repeatedly before beginning his swing. As a younger player I imitated these actions just because I wanted to look like a great man of the game. Not until I was professional and had worried and thought and experimented in trying to improve the games of club members, did I discover that behind these apparent mannerisms were thoughtfully devised routines for assuring correct address, smooth and solid shifting of weight, and the feel of having the club under precise control.

PHYSICAL ABNORMALITIES MISLEADING

There is a danger of misinterpreting stars' peculiarities as elements of universally sound form. Sometimes a player's physical abnormality may mislead others into trying to adopt his style. There's no telling how many hopeful golfers went wrong trying to copy Bob Jones' straight left arm and got so stiffened they could only pound down at the ball instead of swinging and hitting in the powerful, graceful, Jones manner.

Ben Hogan's rare adeptness with his hands indicates rather clearly that a grip identical with his wouldn't necessarily be the most effective grip for a man or woman with average hands. Yet, basically, Hogan's combination of palm- and finger-grip is sound for almost all players. The slight variations from the common standard are thoroughly justified by Hogan's structural and muscular differences.

Snead's own style

Some amazing contortions have resulted from the efforts of players to get their hands as high as Sam Snead does on his backswing. These unsuccessful imitators haven't learned what Snead learned. He found that his arms are longer than normal for a man of his height. Consequently he doesn't teach his pupils to get high at the top of the backswing. He is quite satisfied when their hands go to the point that is normal and comfortable for them.

Again, Snead's abnormal bodywise flexibility enables him to turn a great deal more than the average person can turn, and this automatically raises his hands to a higher point. Should average persons try to turn the same amount, they undoubtedly would lose balance. And, while they wouldn't fall down, once that balance was lost they would instinctively tense or tighten their muscles so that a free, natural swing would be impossible.

Jones and Armour in their writings on golf instruction emphasized the importance of a slight pause at the top of the backswing. Armour noted this pause as one of the few points common to absolutely all great players. Yet every teaching professional has seen many "duffers" who have miserable shots and yet think they are following the advice of Jones and Armour when they hesitate in suspended animation at the points farthest back in their swings. The explanation is that they do not understand that the pause at the top of the backswing is an effect and not a cause.

WEIGHT TRANSFERENCE ESSENTIAL

When weight is properly transferred to the right foot as the body turn is being made in the backswing, the player gets firmly set at the point farthest back in his swing. His hands are bound to stay in that farthest back position for an instant as the downswing begins with the initial action of transferring weight to the left foot.

Of course, if the player starts his downswing incorrectly with a flip of the hands, there is no pause at the top of the backswing. Power is lost from the swing because the premature flip of the hands brings the club into such a position that body action, the source of power, is almost nullified. In endeavoring to protect players against this serious error of premature hand action, authorities have described their feelings while getting the club started down. Chick Evans wrote that when he was hitting the ball well he always had a sensation of "hauling the club down with his left arm." Snead says, "the feeling is like that of pulling a bell rope that extends up over your right shoulder."

These sensations, too, are effects rather than causes. If the player stays back on his right foot in the downswing and consciously strives for the feeling of pulling the club with his left arm and shoulder he never gets into position to hit.

Understanding the Fundamentals

In learning to play good golf the player can't be impressed too much with the fundamentals that (1) the body is the main source of power and (2) the hands are the main factor in precision. Of course there is an element of direction control in body action and some slight degree of power in the hands, but these are secondary. Coordinated action of the body as the power source of the club and the hands as its rudder is the only way of achieving an effective golf swing.

Footwork is the foundation of body action. I have spent many hours of discussion with other pros on the problem of teaching proper foot action to the fat, the lean, the medium, the tall, the short, those of average stature, the young, the middle-aged, and the old. Eventually, I learned that the surest and simplest way of teaching foot action for the proper transference of weight was to make use of the forward press, which the average golfers of a dozen years ago, or longer, regarded as only an eccentric identifying mark of the Scotch-born pros' swing.

In the four steps of procedure by which the player takes his position to the ball, my system places him with his weight favoring his left foot—the way he'll be balanced when he hits the ball.

Key Movements of Footwork

Then the two movements of the forward press and the reverse press are really the key movements of correct footwork. In the first movement—the forward press—the right knee is bent forward a bit more. After that the player makes a reverse press which simply consists of reversing the knee positions. That is, the left knee bends and the right knee straightens. This automatically changes the weight to the right foot. In no case should there be any exaggeration that would tend to lock the knees at any point, nor should the heels be raised off the ground during this one-two operation. In fact, in the case of good golfers this knee action of the forward press becomes so modified that unless one is trained in this highly important requirement, one is apt to overlook it entirely. The second movement—the reverse press—is vital because it's the only way in which the feet work easily in initiating the correct shifting of weight.

Many people trying to learn golf from books or personal lessons repeatedly discover the advice, "sit down a bit to the ball." This admonition to keep the knees slightly bent is given so stiff knees won't prevent good footwork from actuating proper body action and setting solid balance.

Fairly often you see high-scoring golfers who keep their right leg straight on the backswing and think that they are providing themselves with the right sort of an axis for their body turn. They may say they are trying to prevent dipping their right shoulder and digging in behind the ball. Their attempted cure doesn't work because what they really are doing by keeping the right knee stiff is throwing their weight on the left foot in the backswing. With weight thus improperly distributed they can't get the club back in the right manner or get set to swing, so they throw themselves still more out-of-balance in their downswings and pound down at the ball.

Footwork keeps head steady

In learning golf the player generally hears so much about keeping his head still that he almost breaks his neck trying to freeze his head in position. What he must learn is that proper footwork is the basis of balance. If his footwork is correct, his head will be held level without any conscious effort.

The playing star has found by long experimentation and practice the essential relationship between good footwork and good shots. In attaining a "tournament polish" the stars develop footwork to a degree that is beyond the capabilities of other golfers. Snead, Hogan, and Craig Wood, for example, have magnificent foot action and timing in giving a right-foot push that speeds body action and produces the maximum flow of power through the clubhead into the ball. Snead refers to this foot-and-leg action when he tells about getting more distance by giving the ball a "kick."

Bob MacDonald makes a strong point of this footwork in the excellent golf instruction film he produced for the National Golf Foundation to distribute for high school and college golf training. He says that the footwork at the beginning of the downswing is quite similar to footwork in starting a sprint.

One of the many very valuable features of the teaching method of that justly renowned golf instructor Ernest Jones, is the simple manner in which he teaches his pupils how to shift their weight. He ties a knife on the end of a handkerchief and has the pupil swing the handkerchief so the knife will be at the end of the fully extended handkerchief throughout the swing. To keep the knife from being jerked and the handkerchief from flapping, demands smooth transference of weight while maintaining security of balance.

Learn a Little at a Time

A most important principle for you to bear in mind while learning to play good golf is that of not trying to learn too much at once. You possibly have heard many a locker-room jest about the softest touch on a golf course being the fellow who's just had a lesson. Frequently he is, but only because he's tried to learn too much at one time.

The eager student doesn't realize it but, in demanding to be taught more than anyone could absorb in one lesson, he may have injured the reputation of some competent young professional and given the young man a feeling of dismal frustration. The young professional figures that he has handled properly all of the student's major troubles. Yet when he sees his student a few days later on the course, the student is worse than before.

It took me some time as a young professional to discover that there was a definite limit to what I could impart to a pupil in one half-hour lesson so that he would have complete understanding and retention. Realization of that limitation became clear as I spent more time teaching myself for competitive play. When I concentrated on one point in my study and practice, my game showed improvement. When I tried to cover too much territory on the practice tee, my progress was uncertain and slow.

Protect against confusion

At the Bel Air Country Club in California I've had the good fortune to have my pupils say that their opponents pay for the lessons they receive from me. I know that having my teaching system organized so I can concentrate on the one point in the lesson that is most at fault is important. It protects both the pupil and me against confusion and high pressure in attempting to do a major operation on a swing in a half hour.

You will be able to organize your own golf learning and practice for definite and satisfactorily quick improvement of your game if you learn how I happened to organize my system of instruction. In studying the work of successful

instructors in sports other than golf I saw how they organized their teaching by a specific, simple plan.

The football coach has his squad divided for sessions at
tackling, blocking, kicking, passing, ball-carrying and
handling other offensive or defensive assignments. The
baseball coach assigns his men, for certain periods, to
fielding, batting, base-running, throwing, and catching.
Other coaches have their men practicing details for periods that give time enough for the lesson to be fairly well
understood and learned.

Golf practice not hard

Two- or three-hour practice sessions for high-school
athletes are common and these sessions are scheduled
day after day. In baseball spring-training camps the
players have five to eight hours of practice six days a
week and the coaches see that nobody is loafing. In view
of the procedure in other sports isn't it strange that in golf,
which requires a most delicate balance of power and precision, a player who practices more than four hours several days a week is regarded as a superman who submits
to a torturous ordeal to become a champion?

In golf there are comparatively few players who practice at all. And most of them do not have their practice
organized on a basis that gives them some assurance of
benefit. Very few golfers (less than one per cent) take as
many as six lessons a year so they'll know what and how
to practice.

The traditional length of a golf lesson is a half hour.
Why? I don't know. Like many another professional I have
given lessons in locker-room conversation and demonstration that didn't take three minutes and such lessons have
been worth $100 to each of those receiving them although
those lessons didn't cost a cent. I also have given many a
half-hour lesson that was so futile my conscience both-

THE SWING
(Completed position)

This picture illustrates the completed position and the nine that follow illustrate the movements of the swing.

START OF SWING
(Forward press)

Hands are moved slightly forward by slight bending of right knee.

Heels remain on ground.

Reverse knee position from preceding move. This shifts weight
  to right foot and rocks hands slightly to right, putting
  player in position to move club on backswing with a turning motion of the body.

Right knee is not locked.   Heels are still on the ground.

Club still on ground.

Right hand (1) picks up club while simultaneously . . .

Left hand (2) sets club in position with a downward thrust.

This is key action in determining direction. At conclusion of
this action the left arm has assumed natural position:
fairly straight but not stiff.

RAISING CLUB TO TOP OF SWING
(Done with turning of body)

Note prominence of thumb position and how thumbs keep the
club steady without tenseness.

Left arm stays in position while right arm bends into throwing
position.

Right knee is not locked.   Left knee is "thrown" forward.

Turn and rise up on ball of left foot.

Note how head position is brought down from preceding position by both knees being flexed as weight is being shifted to left foot.

Hands keep club in same position throughout swing.
Weight has now been shifted to left side.
Left heel on ground.

Line shows natural turn of body (from right knee to left shoulder) . . . swinging the club through the ball.

Head hasn't turned but has raised as left side straightens.

The right side simultaneously thrusts through pressure on ball
of right foot . . .

As left side pulls the club into the ball.

Hands high.

Fully completed turn with weight on left foot.

*   *   *   *   *   *

This picture and the ten that follow constitute a complete series showing a side view of: THE SWING.

Normal comfortable position of left arm—not tense or stiff.

Note left thumb at 10:30 position on shaft.

Club sole flat on ground.

Left foot opposite ball.

Toes on line parallel to line of shot, weight evenly divided at this point.

Accomplished by relaxing the right knee. This brings right hand to the club as weight shifts to left foot.

At this stage right heel is turned out to a position at a right angle to the line of shot.

Weight is now on left foot.

Weight has been shifted to right foot.

Hands have rocked back to point almost opposite right knee.

Right knee straight but not locked.

Heels both still on ground.

The club is "set" or "cocked" into position by a sharp pickup action of right arm and a simultaneous downward thrust of left arm.

The setting or cocking of the club determines the direction of the shot.

Club has been brought up to top of swing with an easy, natural
 turn of the body.

Left knee "thrown" forward.

Right knee not locked.

Left heel raised off ground.

Weight on right foot.

Weight reshifted to left foot as knees reverse position.

Weight has been completely transferred to left foot.

Body turn now swinging club down and through ball.

Right heel off ground but pressure against right foot inside aids body turn.

Body turn swinging club out on "follow through."
Straight left leg but left knee is not locked.
Note pressure on right foot to add power to body turn.

Full turn of body.
Hands high.
Weight on left foot.

*   *   *   *   *   *

This picture and the five that follow show closeups of the hands throughout the important phases of the swing.

Three knuckles of left hand can be seen by player.

Left thumb at 10:30 position on shaft.

Right thumb at 1:30 position on shaft.

$1\frac{1}{2}$ in.

Hands have rocked forward about 1½ inches

Club remains on ground but it does rotate so that, at this point, face turns "open" slightly.

Hands have moved to a point almost opposite right knee.
Club has rocked back.

Club is still on ground, but reverse rotation has now put face
in a slightly "closed" position.

This illustrates club in perfect position—ready to be raised with body turn.

Pickup with right hand is simultaneous with downward thrust by left hand. This downward thrust has set the club so that (1) shaft is "inside" the intended line of ball flight and (2) the clubface is "square" with ball.

Direction of shot is determined by position of club. Position of club is controlled and determined by the manner in which the left hand actually positions club and this is reflected in position of the left wrist at top of swing.

Note prominence of both thumbs in keeping the club in position without tenseness or "clutching." Hands are in perfect "leverage" position and little finger of right hand is also in perfect position. Note so-called *American Grip* position of left hand. While this picture may invite discussion, it nevertheless portrays the strong hand position at the top of swing.

*   *   *   *   *   *

This picture and the six that follow show that the swing with iron clubs is the same as with wood clubs.

Left arm comfortably straight—not tense.

Grip same as for woods—left thumb at 10:30, right thumb at 1:30.

Weight on left foot, left knee straight but not locked.

Right knee relaxed, right heel turned out. Ball opposite left heel.

IRON SHOT—THE FIRST MOVE
(The forward press)

Hands rock forward about an inch.

Weight on left foot.

Right leg bent slightly, heels stay on ground.

Club head still on ground.

Accomplished by reversing knee position from preceding movement. This shifts weight to right foot and rocks hands slightly to right, placing player in position to move club on backswing with a turning motion of body.

Weight now on right foot, right knee straight but not locked. Both heels still on ground. Club still on ground.

This is the key action and controls not only the direction but also the type of shot. That is, high shot with "stop" or fade or low shot with "run" or hook. Accomplished with a deliberate "pick-up" action (1) with right while simultaneously (2) the left arm with a downward thrust "sets" the club in position. With this action, the club can be "set open" or "set closed" and in turn deliberate slice or hook shots can be produced.

Note prominence of thumb positions and how they keep the
    club steady without tenseness.

Left arm stays in normal position while right arm bends into a
    natural throwing position.

Right knee is not locked, left knee is "thrown" forward.

Left heel and foot raised.

Head position lowered as weight is shifted to left foot through reversing knee action.

Hands keep club in same position as at top of swing. This permits reverse turn of body to swing the club down and through the ball.

Fully completed turn of body with weight on left foot.

*　　　*　　　*　　　*　　　*　　　*

*This picture and the seven that follow show a front view of
the putting stroke.*

Left thumb in normal position on shaft: at 10:30. V pointing to
right shoulder. Club in normal position: face at right angles
to line of putt.

Ball in normal position: at a point opposite the left heel.

Feet: Heels very close together so that no extreme or exaggerated knee action is required to shift weight from one
foot to the other.

Showing how little finger of left hand is curled under the
shaft. Left hand grip is normal in every respect but this.

Purpose of placing little finger in this position is to prevent
tense or tight grip.

It also prevents pronation of clubface—a common fault on
short putts.

Notice overlap of two fingers. This prevents tension in right
hand just as curling little finger of left hand prevents
tension in left hand.

In this grip the sense of clubhead "feel" is concentrated in the
first two fingers and thumb of both hands. This is where
it should be to give delicate control needed in putting.

This grip is much like the regular grip used on all shots. It
includes the same general hand position with the exception of the double-overlap and the curling under of the
little finger of the left hand.

PUTTING
(Completed position)

Hands are in same general position as is used in all shots with
the exception of a double-overlap and the undercurling
of little finger of left hand.

Heels are close together. Weight on left foot at start of shot.

Club is in normal position: shaft tilted slightly, clubface at
right angles to line of putt.

Ball is in same general position: opposite left heel.

PUTTING
(Start of backswing)

Weight has shifted to right foot.

Hands have "set" or "cocked" the club for the swing.

Club is cocked in normal position: face of club being "set" square with intended line of shot.

This determines "aim" and "direction."

Club has been swung back with delicate, almost imperceptible, motion of body.

Hands keep club as it was at outset of swing and body turn gives true pendulum swing to the stroke.

Note the clubhead still square with line of putt.

Swing of body reflected in action of knees. *Compare this with preceding picture.* This body motion determines intensity of hit and with very little practice player can get feel of force with which ball should be stroked.

Note that hand position remains exactly the same.

Knees have returned to original starting position.

Clubface still square with line of shot as it is being swung
forward with turn of body.

Note that hands have kept club "square" with line of shot. This insures direction, while distance is controlled with body turn or "swing."

*　　*　　*　　*　　*　　*

*This picture and the four that follow show a rear-view of the
putting stroke.*

Club is in normal position: face square with line.

Ball is opposite left heel.

Feet are close together.

Weight has been delicately shifted to right foot. Compare distances between club shaft and right knee.

Club has been cocked or set for the swing.

Clubface square with line of shot.

Club has been swung away from ball with almost imperceptible turn of body. Note slight change in knee.

Clubface has been kept square with line of putt.

Body turn has brought club back to ball with pendulum action while hands have kept clubface in perfectly square position so that positive directional control is maintained.

Body has swung club through ball with perfect pendulum
action—and even at this point, clubface still remains almost square with line of shot.

⁂ ⁂ ⁂ ⁂ ⁂ ⁂

The picture above and the six that follow it show the proper method of playing a ball out of a very bad lie with a No. 7 iron.

This illustrates how ball would be placed if it were in a good lie.

These are the normal foot, club, and hand positions.

Foot, hand and body positions are same as in normal shot but
ball is played back at a point more opposite right heel.
Club is, therefore, tilted forward and down on the ball.

Weight has been shifted to right foot and club has been started with hands so that it is "set" or "cocked" for the swing.

Turn of body has moved club up and around to top of swing.

Hands have kept club in position: "square with ball."

Left arm is natural, straight, without tension.

Weight is back on right heel; right knee is naturally straight
but not "locked" or tense.

Reverse turn of body bringing club down and through ball. Weight has been shifted to left foot and natural, full, free swing is being made while hands are free to keep club in position and in line with shot.

Body has brought club down and is now going on through into
  natural finish.

Club automatically digs down into grass and brings ball out.

This low position of arms is typical of trouble shots which are played "off the right foot."

Clubface is kept square with direction throughout swing.

* * * * * *

This picture and the four that follow show how the ball should be played out of a sand trap on a short, 40-yard shot.

This is normal position used on all shots.

Position of ball in sand trap in relation to the normal position is also shown.

Ball is at a point nearly opposite right heel.

Club correspondingly tilted forward so hands are above a point opposite left heel. Note dotted line.

Weight was shifted to right foot, club was set or "cocked" into
position and then a natural turn of the body brought the
club up and around to the top of the swing.

Note the usual features of the normal swing:
1. Weight on right foot.
2. Straight left arm.
3. Club square with line of shot.

Normal reverse turn of body swings club down on the ball, into the sand, and then naturally carries it on into the follow through.

Intensity of body turn determines how hard ball is to be hit.

Hands establish club position and thereby determine and control direction.

The closeness of the ball to the right foot is determined by the amount of "sand" that will be taken; or if play is in grass, how much divot will be taken.

Note how sand was contacted when shot was played.

*　　　*　　　*　　　*　　　*　　　*

This picture and the three that follow show the cut shot used to raise the ball sharply to clear a bank in a sand trap.

This shot is the same as a deliberately played slice used to produce high-flying shots. (This is the reason why some players have no trouble in sand traps.)

BALL is played at a point forward or opposite left toe rather than back, opposite right heel as suggested in previous shot. Club shaft is perpendicular, as in slice shots, with toe "turned in" at start.

FEET should be placed as follows: right foot in slightly advanced or forward position, while left remains in normal position.

Note characteristics common to slice shots:

WEIGHT OF BODY: tends to "list" toward left foot. This is
due to fact that right foot is in advanced position and,
therefore, restricts body turn and causes this "list" toward
left foot. Position of arms: very high and upright.

CLUB: definitely an open position. This, of course, was
planned. In this shot left wrist has definite inward turn
towards body. The result of these characteristics will be a
natural cut across and under the ball—which is the desired
effect.

Club has come down and across the line of flight, and has cut down under the ball to give it the desired "lift" or high flight.

SAND TRAP CUT SHOT
(The deliberate slice)

Notice the high position of the club at the finish. This is typical
  of these shots.

Notice how club contacted ball at proper spot and how it
  scooped out the sand as it cut across and came on through.

* * * * * *

A golf class at U.C.L.A. lined up for swing practice. The author and his assistant, Glen Dunlap are in the foreground demonstrating the swing for the class.

ered me when I took the lesson fee. It was this sting of conscience as well as the ambition to advance in my profession that impelled me to develop my system of teaching.

What I teach is fundamentally what almost every other successful golf instructor teaches. I think that there are only two routines in my system that may be debated to any extent by other professionals who teach. These are (1) having the right foot at 90 degrees to the line of intended flight, at address; and (2) coordinating the right-hand lift with the downward thrust of the left hand at an early stage of the backswing. Later I'll explain more fully the validity of these details which I have found to be essential in the expert golfer's form.

Eight Steps Are the Same

But what the system has done that most golfers need is to organize teaching and learning on a basis of only eight simple steps. These eight steps are common to all American golfers who've become famous during the past quarter century. In a few respects, the order of the routine is changed in the play of the stars and to an even lesser extent are there departures from these basic steps. In each case, when variation does occur it has to be compensated for by an unnecessary action that involves an element of needless risk. I think that Sam Snead went to the root of sound golf when he said, at an instruction clinic of the Professional Golfers' Association, "I try to swing in the most simple way."

In determining "the most simple way" there are only two departments of research: the body for power and the hands for direction.

Theoretically, golf should be made easier than other popular sports by the fact that the ball remains in place while the golfer moves. In other popular outdoor sports both the ball and the players move. The theory is blasted by the fact that the moving ball keeps players in such rapid motion that there is not the danger that the conscious mind will interfere with what should be spontaneous, naturally coordinated motions.

One-armed men, one-legged men, puny or fat people, or perfect physical specimens, all play rather good golf. So, logically, it is not differences in physical qualifications but in mental attitude that account for a lot of the wide variation in golf proficiency. The failure to attain the right mental attitude for learning and playing the game is due, mainly, to inability to think of one's swing as an organized procedure. The alibi is given: "I can't think of a dozen details while I'm making a swing; when I try to, I get everything snafued." This alibi, in itself, is evidence of failure to organize the swing and the thinking. Certainly, the four routine actions in taking position to the ball involve no complications. They are performed while there is no requirement of timing or complexity of "man in motion."

Swing simply organized

The forward and reverse press, the two initial procedures of the swing, are done with the club on the ground (except in cases of shots in traps where the rules prohibit grounding the club); the hand-positioning action of the right and left hands is a somewhat delicate but not complicated performance. For the rest of the swing nature takes its course, since everything has been set for natural, free body turn and controlling the clubface with the hands.

What is so confusing about the eight simple steps that they should call for any strain on the mind?

Physical educators properly make quite a point of the social values of golf and the temperamental discipline of the game. To the one who has learned to simplify and organize thinking of the swing, the game has the additional value of reminding its players to use a similar mental approach to other problems: First simplify as to the essentials, then organize. After I have asserted that golf is a natural game, there may be criticism that my system produces a synthetic rather than spontaneous game. But, because this division of the address and swing into merely eight steps gets the swing "back to nature," I can reconcile theory and practice.

While instructing the students at the University of California in Los Angeles, I have seen how the learning attitude helps one to learn good golf quickly. The students have been conditioned to the learning attitude by an exceptionally competent staff of instructors in the usual college courses. Then, when they come to me, they want to learn and they expect to be taught.

Attitude for learning

At the lesson tee of the golf club there is too much of a subconscious attitude of wanting to be taught and not enough wanting to learn—unless the learning can be acquired quickly and painlessly. I can understand why that condition prevails. Many of those who take golf lessons are very successful businessmen. It is instinctive for them to feel that some young man who may have caddied for them ten years ago can't teach them anything about anything. I've seen any number of cases in which the businessman student takes the play away from the professional golf teacher, then wonders why the lesson has been so unproductive.

The instructor must put across, subtly, his responsibility, his fitness, and his dominance. Armour does this with astute psychology—by sitting in the shade of an umbrella, having a caddy tee the practice balls, and making sage and constructive comment on the pupil's swing. But I do not have Armour's grand gift of showmanship as a psychological asset. So I rely on impressing the pupil with the fact that the golf swing is a thoughtfully organized system of positions and procedures. The American businessman is a great admirer of system. Hence I get in him a mood for learning by interesting him in seeing how a system works and in giving it a trial.

Pupil helps himself

It is important that the pupil learn, instead of merely being taught with the risk that the educational influence from the outside quickly vanish. Therefore, I go into detail to make each action clearly understood by the pupil. He participates in the lesson by helping to teach himself.

For instance, when I come to the fourth step in taking position and have the pupil turn the right heel outward so it is at 90 degrees to the direction line, the pupil may question this detail. The pupil probably has noticed that quite a few of the fine players have the right toe pointed slightly backward at address. There also is a disposition among older students to think that the right toe pointed outward will help them get an easier and fuller body turn to compensate for the stiffness of their years away from athletic activity.

Then I explain that the structure of the hip socket is such that turning the right toe out has a tendency to lock or restrict the free turn of the right side of the body. If you take that freedom out of the swing, you can't make it up by trying to come around with the left side.

Many of the star players will assume a right-toe-out position to overcome the tendency to hook the ball or knock it off to the left. They get so much action in the clubhead that the club runs away with them. They have to set up a restraining action to keep the clubhead in the path. The ordinary player with this right-toe-out position would be very much inclined to develop a slice. Actually, what happens to the strong free swinger who puts his right toe out is that he sets up a bit of a slice stance to overcome the risk of hooking.

WHAT'S HOGAN'S SECRET?

At the 1947 Ryder Cup matches at Portland, Oregon, Ben Hogan said, "Joe, I've finally learned to play golf." I said, "That's quite a confession from a star. What's been the change?" He told me that he had learned to fade the ball. I didn't have the chance then to inquire into details and later, as Ben was having the greatest competitive year any of the headliners ever had, I didn't get a chance to query him. Ben won 10 of the 12 summer tournaments he played in 1948.

There have been a thousand guesses about the secret Hogan discovered that will, according to some stories, "go into the box" with him. Now I'll make my guess. There are only two ways in which a fade or a slice can be produced. The same is true of a hook. One is by adjusting the grip, with the right hand a bit more on top and the left hand a bit more in front of the club. This would open the club and a slice would be bound to occur. But this would sacrifice length and neither Hogan nor anybody else wants to sacrifice length. They can't do that and get on the green to score birdies and eagles.

The other method of getting a fade is by adjusting the foot position, advancing the right foot slightly so the swing, while not impeded in any way, will be just a wee bit outside-in. My observation of Hogan's play later convinced me that this adjustment in his stance was what had accounted for his controlled fade. Jimmy Stewart, the motion picture star, made the same adjustment which was prescribed for him when he developed a chronic hook. The change worked wonders for Jimmy, but it didn't quite get him into Hogan's class. Jimmy is about an 80 golfer and I'm proud of him as a pupil. He got his game started on an organized basis with my system and keeps it consistent although he doesn't play as often as he would like.

DISCOVERING AND CURING A FAULT

The experienced professional has learned that there's a wide difference between analyzing a fault and curing it. The cure requires a simple explanation that the pupil can understand clearly and apply without too much difficulty. My colleagues in the Professional Golfers' Association, in their frank discussions on instruction problems, say that most professionals who have been teaching five to ten years have become pretty good analysts. But, they also say that the time, study, and genius demanded in getting the pupil to effect a cure from correct diagnosis are what determine the rating of a professional as a successful instructor.

This problem of getting the pupil to understand is rooted in the inability of the muscles to hear and the pupil's lack of understanding of the elemental phases of the swing. This lack of basic understanding is going to be diminished as more youngsters get the right start at golf in classes conducted by professionals at clubs and in schools. Now the professional seldom gets an adult who has been started in the game by having the swing fully explained. The professionals' adult customers on the lesson tee are patients rather than students. They're seeking the cure for some fault acquired over the years. And, of course, they want the cure to work quickly.

In organizing my system of golf instruction, the prime objective was to make it possible for the golfer to do something to help himself. Each shot will be played with an understanding of the simple fundamentals of foot, leg, body, arm, and hand action so that, when he does go wrong, he will be able to reason out the cause of his trouble logically. Much of the time he will be able to do this and will continue to play with increased enjoyment. I believe that there are as many who have quit golf because of the monotony of unsatisfactory scores as there are golfers now playing.

If the golfer could play with a professional instructor during each round and apply the teaching under expert supervision, decided scoring ability would be inevitable on every stroke. But that's impossible. Much of everyone's golf must be learned by himself, regardless of the talents of his professional and the frequency of his lessons. Having an organized routine of instruction makes this responsibility of learning easier on the one who wants to learn and makes the responsibility of effective teaching easier on the professional.

There is so much art, individuality, and finesse involved in perfecting a golf swing that there is need of very capable instructors. Often the golfer doesn't do what he thinks he is doing. I find this true with those who are using my simple system, just as the expert players learn when some other experts look over their swings and discover variation between intent and performance in a detail of body or hand action.

If and when the completely perfect, all-applicable method of teaching golf is evolved, it won't do away with teachers any more than the evolution of religions has eliminated work for clergymen.

Easier learning routine

The most urgent task in golf is to make it easier for golfers to learn. Generally the teaching has progressed soundly and far. There's not the variation you might expect among the lessons of those who are acknowledged by professionals to be master instructors.

My system has taken the few major points from all resultful golf instruction that are common to the great playing exponents of golf, organized these points into an orderly routine and given them to the student as a simple, understandable basis for his game.

Very soon the student will learn from this system that anything he tries to do unnaturally is almost invariably faulty. Take, for example, the effort of many a high-handicap golfer to keep his right elbow in close to his side. As a matter of fact, the right elbow of a star doesn't stay close to his right side in the back swing; when the left side straightens as the downswing begins, the body shift brings the right elbow in close. This body shift and downswing also bring the right shoulder down in what so many "duffers" believe is a bad fault—ducking the shoulder, but which actually is a natural and desirable action in a proper swing.

In a misunderstood attempt to deliberately bring the right elbow close to the side in the backswing, the high-scoring golfer usually stiffens his left arm and rolls his right wrist under so far that he will make it impossible to hit the ball squarely. Also he will probably keep his weight mainly on his left leg so he can't shift into position to swing at the ball. Thus, in a foggy effort to force something that comes naturally with correct grip and body swing, the struggling golfer has developed two or three serious faults, any one of which would have ruined his swing.

WHY YOUNG "WONDERS" FAIL

Many of us have seen young golfers who were wonders as boys or girls but who didn't keep up to their early promise. A lot of guesses are made to explain the failure of these youngsters to develop. It has been my observation that when they get to the point where they have to think about what they're doing they don't know where and how to start. They make bewildered experiments, all of which get them away from the swings that came naturally to them as children. Mounting scores blot out the incentive to keep at the game, so they turn to other amusements.

These youngsters picked up golf but never learned to learn it. The same condition prevails among many older golfers who score between 90 and 110 and have philosophically resigned themselves to bad golf because they need the exercise of walking.

No one in the past ten years of the application of my eight-step system has failed to improve decidedly after a few lessons. And this isn't because there is anything at all mysterious or revolutionary about the mechanical phases of the system. It is simply because I have made it easy for these people to think correctly about their posi tion to the ball, the body action to swing the club, and the use of the hands in maintaining the clubface in the desired position for a straight ball, a hook, or a slice.

A little thinking rather than any tiring muscular work has accounted for cutting 15 to 20 strokes off the games of men and women who were embarrassed, discouraged, and hopeless about their golf. It would have been no use to tell them to "concentrate" in making their shots. They didn't know what to concentrate on. The presentation and explanation of a system that could be used effectively by those who were willing to make a habit of eight successive steps brought an organized plan of golf within their capabilities.

Not enough right hand

Most of these pupils who graduated from the high handicaps into very satisfactory scores didn't know how to use their right hand. I've never been able to learn to my own satisfaction why this was true. But, I suspect that the average person who plays golf has read or heard so much about left-hand control of the club, dragging the club away with the left hand, and the "straight left" that they became left-hand "punchy." *The tendency to slice (which is already strong enough because of failure to shift weight to the right foot in making the body turn of the backswing) is further magnified by the left hand alone trying to handle the club.*

I have found that the third step in my swing routine clears away this left-hand confusion, but I must say that it is the only step that the pupils find difficult to master. The pupil has to understand that the hands must work together and in conjunction with body power which is transmitted by the arms. The logical position for exercising precise control of the clubface is that in which the left hand is closer to the body and higher up on the shaft. The right hand must be adjusted to the left so both hands will remain in correct, diametrically opposed positions and will work uniformly for the purposes of power and control.

The pushdown by the left hand should occur with the simultaneous slight lift of the right when the club in the backswing is on the line about a foot away from the ball. This will spontaneously provide all the extension of the left arm needed for a correct swing and will extend the left arm naturally in a strong position without stiffening it.

In helping the pupil to teach himself the happy medium between the stiff left arm and the sloppy left, this detail of left- and right-hand counteraction in the backswing does the job easily and without risking the danger of getting the whole left side out of proper adjustment.

It is a natural method that very effectively cultivates a keen feeling of hand action that the average golfer usually lacks.

Positioning the club before swinging

I make it plain to my pupils that this routine of hand action occurs earlier in the swing than it would seem to in the case of good golfers. *But I definitely want my pupils, and all golfers, to know how to get the proper feel and position of the club before they swing it.* And, in the case of the better or experienced golfers, the hand and body action occurs, in effect, more or less simultaneously so that the hand action, or cocking of the club, appears to occur later in the backswing. The star can do this but the beginner must benefit by first working the club into the desired position before swinging it.

The pupil also finds it easy to understand and retain the logic of this routine: i.e., getting the hands to perform their function of adjusting the club properly and also getting in position to transmit power to the club with a smoothly accelerating throw coordinated with body action.

To get quicker, more understandable results in this learning process, it is necessary for the pupil to understand the component parts or actions that constitute the whole, and so the part the hands play is, necessarily, explained separately.

Once this is understood, the pupil can coordinate his movements so that the swing or stroke can be made smoothly and "in one piece," as is so often recommended.

One thing that has greatly confused aspiring golfers is what they've heard and read about wrist-cocking at about hip-height on the backswing and also at a lower position, as the hitting zone is entered, on the downswing. The professional can't blame the pupil for being baffled as these instructions, which are easily written or given orally, call for a nicety of timing that the expert sometimes finds very troublesome.

Many ordinary golfers, unable to cock their wrists as the experts do, either swing with frozen wrists or cock their wrists at the top of the swing in an awkward and uncertain action. In neither case can the club be swung through the ball with freedom and steadily increasing speed. Generally, the golfer's action in cocking his wrists incorrectly throws the club out-of-line to the ball and wrecks his balance.

When the pupil understands that the wrist cocking is to lengthen the arc of clubhead travel as well as keep the clubface in desired relation to the path away from and to the ball, most of the confusion is eliminated.

Needless fear of swaying

Another matter that often makes it difficult for the high-handicap player to turn his body properly and get a good swing is his fear of swaying, or coming back straightaway from the ball with his weight on his right leg. He gets so careful he either stays on his left leg, which makes it impossible to turn and shift his weight, or he stands upright and hacks without any leg work or body turn.

The pupil has to learn that a certain amount of sway to the right is inevitable as weight is transferred to the right foot in the backswing. Carefully measure action pictures of the stars and, by comparing body and head position with some fixed object in the background, you will see evidence of what golfers call "swaying."

Eddie Williams, winner of several Professional Golfers' Association senior titles, helps his pupils to get over fear of a sway by telling them that the backswing consists of a lateral shift to the right, then a turn of the body. This, of course, is just what happens with the reverse press followed by a swing in my system.

Search for power

The majority of golfers want to get more distance and will engage in almost any weird experiment to get longer shots. Their only hope of realizing this end lies in learning that power comes from the body. With the forward and backward press initiating the proper body turn and making retention of balance quite certain, the player can swing at the ball with maximum speed. Hand action, he must understand, keeps the club in line so the head comes squarely in contact with the ball. That's about all the hands have to do with power. As I have mentioned previously, the function of the hands is comparable to that of a clutch, or differential, in an automobile.

The pupil also must learn that in the short-approach shots the body must move smoothly in good balance; this is regardless of what he may have believed about these approaches being entirely hand and/or arm performances. Unless the body turns in easy grace, there is strong risk of arm-and-hand action being so stiff that the approaches can't be hit crisply.

Learning how to "read" the course and the greens so that strokes can be correctly aimed and played with the right force is also a "must" in the curriculum of the golfer. The ordinary golfer loses several strokes in almost every round by not thinking in advance about where a ball can be stroked within the limit of his capabilities.

There are many fine golf instructors on the roster of the Professional Golfers' Association; some of them of national fame and others whose reputations, based on results, are known only within their own districts. They can teach competently but whether they teach effectively depends very much on the pupil's attitude toward learning.

When you realize that you must *learn* golf and begin by understanding the whys and wherefores, you can quickly think your way to better golf on an organized plan of stroke making.

5

Golf Instruction in the School Program

GOLF INSTRUCTION IN HIGH SCHOOLS AND COLLEGES HAS expanded tremendously during the past ten years. More than 60 universities and prep schools have their own courses; a number of them of national championship character.

Athletic directors and other physical educators and school administrative staffs have been giving golf prominence on the sports programs because it brings into participation students who can't "make the team" in other sports, and gives the members of those teams a sport in which they too can be active long after they have left school.

The many years during which one can play good golf and the game's handicapping feature which puts opponents on an equal competitive basis are features of golf which particularly endorse the game to physical educators. Due to the popularity of the game among older Americans, the value of golf in making social and business contacts is a practical factor in developing proficiency in the game. This is also considered by those who plan a sports

99

program that will have a substantial carry-over value for students after graduation.

The increase in municipal golf courses, their tie-ups with high school golf instruction and play schedules, and the encouragement private clubs are giving to high school and college golf enthusiasts as potential replacements of older members, have given impetus to the spread of golf in schools.

And, for those young players who respond to the challenge and opportunities of championship competition, there are many district and national junior championships in addition to the state-wide high school championships in most states. The largest of all golf championships is the boys' national tournament conducted by the Junior Chamber of Commerce. Fifteen thousand boys have competed in state qualifying rounds of this event.

More Competition for Juniors

Under the auspices of golf associations, girls' championships are growing steadily. Since the war, the United States Golf Association has conducted a national championship for girls and the Women's Western Golf Association has revived its girls' annual championship. It is not unusual for a girl to play as a member of a high school team. Some years ago Helen Hicks, who later won the American women's national championship, starred as a member of a high school team in the New York metropolitan district.

Part of the problem of the golf program in schools is that, about the time school vacations occur, the golf season is reaching its height in the northern and central states. This curtails school arrangement and supervision of outdoor play, but it has the advantage of keeping the golf students together for instruction and practice.

The primary objectives of the college and high school golf-education program are to give the pupils clear understanding of the fundamentals of the game and the stroke, and to give them the lasting good habits of a sound swing. Many professionals with considerable experience in teaching university and high school students have found this can be done as well, and perhaps better, indoors as outside.

Outdoors the pupils are mainly interested in seeing how far they can make the ball travel and are inclined to make unwise experiments that undo the teaching of sound golf form. When good golf form is established the pupils have assurance of utmost distance as well as control. Indoor initial training also makes it easier to get the young people to attend to the details of the short game.

PROFESSIONAL HELP IN PLANNING

In planning and arranging indoor instruction facilities in a gymnasium or field house it is advisable to consult one or several experienced golf professionals. They are acquainted with the type of facilities that will be the best investment of the funds available and are sharply aware of the safety factor that must always be considered where clubs are being swung and hard golf balls are in flight. The professional's advice on the number and type of new or used clubs to be used in school instruction also will be very helpful.

Because a considerable number of the members of the Professional Golfers' Association having been on physical education staffs of universities and high schools as full-time or part-time golf instructors, and because the majority of professionals conduct junior classes at their clubs, the professionals are well-qualified to work competently and in fullest cooperation with physical education department heads who are desirous of making golf instruction a popular and helpful element of the physical education program.

By getting in touch with Professional Golfers' Association officials and members who are located near the school, arrangements can be made for free lectures and demonstrations to get the program under way. It often is possible to have playing stars who are members of golf-goods manufacturers' advisory staffs visit the school for instructive demonstrations and consultation by physical education department members and students. Bookings of these visits may be made through local professionals or directly with the sales departments of the manufacturers with whom the playing stars are associated.

EQUIPMENT FOR INSTRUCTION

In equipping the gymnasium for indoor instruction and practice it is highly desirable to have practice nets and rubber or cocoa mat tees so regulation golf balls can be used and conditions of actual play approximated. If a net or nets can't be aquired, a large piece of canvas suspended from the ceiling will serve as a backstop into which balls can be hit. In this case there should be a foot or more of the canvas on the floor to prevent topped balls going through to the wall. It is also imperative that pupils not be allowed to have tee positions too near the sides of the canvas; preventing the risk of shots hit too much to the right or left missing the canvas and rebounding with danger to the pupil or others in the vicinity.

For instruction and practice in approach and chip shots, a wrestling mat may be used with safety.

The cocoa tee mats wear quickly under the heavy traffic of school instruction and for that reason mats made of used tire casings are being widely installed. These are the same type of mats used extensively on outdoor tees at public courses. There is another artificial tee material of tough fibre that holds the ball in what approximates a lie on grass. This material wears long but is somewhat expensive.

For safe indoor practice there are the knitted yarn balls and a newer ball made of plastic. The latter is hollow and has holes in it to accentuate hooks or slices. In using these balls the floor of the gymnasium should be protected against club damage; this is done by hitting the balls from a tee of composition board such as is used in buildings.

In issuing clubs and balls to students a record should be kept so responsibility is assumed for return of the equipment.

Reprocessed and repainted golf balls may be bought from manufacturers or the used ball dealers who supply driving ranges.

In providing clubs for students' use the stock should provide the brassie (No. 2 wood) for study and practice of the drives and long fairway shots, the midiron (No. 2 iron) for long fairway shots, the mashie (No. 5 iron) for higher trajectory shorter shots from the fairway and for run-up approaches, the mashie-niblick (No. 7 iron) for lofted approaches, pitches and trouble shots, and the putter.

An assortment of weights and lengths to fit students of different builds is needed. When the school budget for the golf program is very low, local professionals may be able to locate used clubs that can be bought cheaply. The shafts of some of these clubs may be cut down by the professional and regripped to be used by shorter students. And although the fit, lie, and balance of these altered clubs will be far from what the professional would recommend in fitting a new set to a purchaser, the cut-down clubs will be adequate for elementary education in golf.

Indoor putting facilities

Indoor putting surface should be provided. Used carpeting with an underlay is usually employed. This helps slow the speed of the ball to that similar on a green and assures a level surface. There are composition surfaces made specially for this purpose. Several styles of putting practice cups are manufactured and may be bought from professionals at almost any golf club.

It is desirable to have many putting areas because the students will naturally engage in enough competition to keep themselves keenly interested in study and practice of this highly important phase of the game. For this activity regular golf balls are essential. It also is advisable to have regular golf balls for study and practice of the short-approach shots. The somewhat delicate timing and "feel" of these shots calls for contact with a real golf ball.

One of the developments in school golf instruction that is bound to grow is the installation of golf practice ranges. The Universities of Minnesota and New Mexico have installed these ranges; they not only provide attractive and large outdoor practice facilities for University students and faculty members at low rates, but they also receive income from non-university golfers. The patronage of these establishments indicates that they are financially sound additions to university sports facilities.

Details of golf driving-range design and construction are given in a book which is published by the National Golf Foundation of Chicago, an organization sponsored by leading makers of golf equipment and operated for the promotion of the game.

In planning golf education there must be kept in balance explanatory lectures, demonstrations, group and individual instruction and supervised practice, indoor and outdoor competition. Marked progress has been made in devising organized and effective programs as golf professionals at universities and high schools have exchanged ideas with coaches in other sports and physical education specialists.

APPRAISING THE PUPILS

The problem of the golf professional is viewed understandingly by the other physical educators. Most of the golf professional's teaching must be done among those who are not especially apt, physically. At clubs the professional's pupils generally are men and women who are not otherwise athletically engaged and, in the case of businessmen, are rushed for time, have had muscular response dulled by sedentary living, and often have their minds burdened by matters far from a golf course. With the youngsters, the professional quite often has the problem of making a good golfer of a boy or girl who has shown no aptitude for any other sport. This is uncommon in most sports since coaches generally have material that has revealed some proficiency or at least a burning determination.

Consequently, the golf professional is eager to get ideas from the work of others who have been successful in physical training, and to adapt these ideas in his own coaching. One of the most interesting of these ideas that has come to my attention was the result of discussion with Wayne Timberman who was a golf professional and school teacher in Indianapolis, and who had a rhythm band for children.

Timberman applied the cadence idea of the rhythm band to the golf positioning and swing routines and quickly developed some excellent swings among eight- and nine-year-old pupils. When the rhythm or cadence count is associated with certain positions of the swing, it is helpful as a reminder to take the steps of the swing in order; but simply as an aid to timing and grace in the swing I haven't found that it helps at all.

Avoid Too Much Talk

One thing that is to be guarded against in school golf instruction is too much talking. The students are interested in action. The best thing that can be done during positioning and swing instruction is to make the initial statements clear and concise, then let the pupils take the action as the talk is repeated. Then a fuller explanation of the step in the routine may be given, after which the students swing again. The instructor then may go through the class correcting individuals and noting those who could be brought in front of the class for a demonstration of the correct method.

Be Careful About Safety

In setting up a class in which there is to be swinging of clubs, by all means take care to have much more room between pupils than you might at first think necessary for safety's sake. Have the first row of pupils line up and take distance. They should do this by holding the club in the right hand, extending it out to the right side a safe distance from the pupil to the right, then take at least two steps to the left.

You can also have pupils in lines in back of the first line, but only when they are standing a safe distance from the person in front of them. They can make sure of the proper distance by holding their club out in front of themselves.

That's about the minimum spacing for safety. An even better way is to have the pupils so far apart that those in the second row will be in a line safely behind but in positions between pupils in the first row. Alternate spacing of lines according to this arrangement is a good plan.

In my teaching at the University of California I arrange outdoor classes where there is plenty of room so the two lines can face each other with a lot of safety margin in all directions. This arrangement allows the two lines to view each other's performances alternately according to the routine of my system, and noting the correctness or error of the pupil opposite.

At UCLA I give five lessons before the pupils hit a ball. The reason for this is that I want them to have a good elemental knowledge of the game and the swing so they will be able to "think golf" for themselves instead of merely acting as images or marionettes of the instructor.

Many times during my instruction of adults at golf clubs I've seen that they are badly handicapped by lack of understanding of the game's elements. Some of them would be much better off if they could go back and start all over again. The bad habits they acquired before they understood the game acquired such a strong hold that the professional can hadly break them.

Dramatize Lectures

By starting at the beginning the school students of golf are protected against many errors. And yet, in giving them this protection with lectures, one must be sure the lectures are interesting, dramatic, and personalized rather than recitals of historical and technical facts. There are several 16 mm. sound motion pictures that can be borrowed from prominent golf club and golf ball manufacturers that fit very well into school golf programs. The National Golf Foundation also has a sound slide-film series on the history, etiquette, swing instruction, and rules of golf.

Unfortunately, among the multitude of books on golf there isn't a really comprehensive history of the game. Frank G. Menke's *Encyclopedia of Sports* contains a brief and accurate historical background of the game. *The Encyclopaedia Britannica* also has a good outline of golf history. Entertaining and instructive books on American golf history by H. B. Martin, Chick Evans, and Charles B. MacDonald are, unfortunately, out of print. Local libraries and book dealers usually can supply enough source material for a lively and informative talk on the background and development of the game.

My usual procedure is to explain, in the first five sessions, the origin of the game and the factors which established its basic character, the game itself and a few points of course design, the rules of the game which are based on playing the ball as it lies, the etiquette of golf, the reasons for the differences in design of the various clubs, and the swing.

In lecturing on the swing I break it up into its few essentials, explain how the swing has to be made to unite the essentials of power and direction, and show how the body controls the distance and the hands the direction. In this part of the training I begin to let the pupils hold a club and swing it, and question them to see if they have absorbed the rudiments.

In the earlier lectures I particularly try to introduce numerous names and incidents, some of them personal, in endeavoring to arouse the feeling of keen interest in the game as an expression of personalities rather than something involving clubs, a ball, some grass, and a way to get school credits in physical education.

According to results at the University of California at Los Angeles my eight-step system is exceptionally well-suited to school golf instruction because all the pupils "get into the act." They check each other's performance in each of the eight routine procedures and by knowing how, where, and why to look for significant actions in the positioning and body and hand action of others, get training in checking their own performances.

Pupils Check Each Other's Efforts

Notwithstanding the simplicity of the system, it is too much to expect that the pupils quickly will develop unerring capacity for checking performance. The speed of the golf swing and the mystifying deviations in shifting weight, as well as the difficulty of inspecting coordinated action of hands, present conditions that require the eye of an expert. But the common, major elements of good form are, for the most part, fairly well checked by other students. This checking helps develop a community of interest and a sort of a team spirit which isn't the easiest thing to encourage in a game as individualized as golf.

After the introductory lectures and demonstrations I take the students into the details of the grip, the stance, lining up the ball, and the swing elements in detail.

The finesse of teaching comes in when one has to instill the "why" of each action into the minds of the pupils instead of letting them start when they don't understand what they are supposed to do. I was impressed with the importance of this matter by being told of the method of development of one of our fine women players, Mrs. Estelle Lawson Page.

Mrs. Page's father, Dr. Lawson, long has been a noted physical educator. He was a versatile athlete himself and became very much interested in golf when he saw a lot of the best type played at the famous old golfing resort, Pinehurst, North Carolina. As Dr. Lawson and his daughter watched the professional and amateur stars they made notes of salient details of form and style. The doctor was very methodical in his research and analysis, and as each note concerning some feature of a player's stance, grip, and action was written down, inquiry was made as to the reason for the detail. Estelle learned more golf than she had taught to her and she's kept a very good game, although her domestic duties are such that she now plays only intermittently.

WRITTEN EXAMINATIONS HELPFUL

To make sure that the students understand their work, and to look for details in which my teaching may be inadequate, I hold periodical written examinations.

The questions, and my own comment on the correct answers follow:

1. *What golf experience have you had prior to taking this course?*

This tips me off to those who have played quite frequently. By watching them I can see if they have basic errors in their swings that should be eliminated by the substitution of proper swing habits.

2. *What is the place of golf in the physical education program?*

I want them to realize that this course isn't for killing time and having fun at a sport, but to acquire a sports ability that will be enjoyable and valuable to them for many years to come.

3. *What is the one basic rule in the game of golf?*

The basic rule is to play the ball as it lies. The exceptions are (a) lost ball, (b) ball out-of-bounds, and (c) unplayable lie.

4. *What influence or effect does the above rule have on golf clubs?*

Playing the ball as it lies necessitates various clubs to produce different effects. For example: straight-faced woods and irons for distance where shots of low trajectory go farther; loft-faced clubs for high shots for position or for getting down under balls that are in bad lies; and the putter for rolling shots on the green or short grass adjacent to the putting green.

5. *What are the two objectives in playing a golf shot?*
(a) Distance, and (b) direction.

6. *What is the determining factor in controlling the direction of a ball in flight?*
Position of the club. A straight ball results from the clubface being square to the ball, a hook results from the clubface being closed to the ball and a slice results from the clubface being open. This positioning of the club is done with the hands. The "dub" does it unintentionally and the expert does it deliberately.

7. *Where does the power, or distance force, come from in a golf shot?*
From rotation of the body. A quarter turn of the body means a quarter swing; a half turn a half swing, and a full turn a full swing. Snead claims his flexibility gives him more power because he can make more of a body turn. This is true of all long hitters and accounts for small men, such as Hogan, or women such as Babe Didrikson Zaharias, being able to hit a ball longer than those who seem to be stronger.

8. *What causes a player to hit behind or top a ball?*
Improper footwork which throws the pivot or rotation of body off-center so that reverse turn of the body and return of the club is high enough to top the ball or low enough to hit the ground behind the ball, according to the way in which the weight has been shifted from one leg to the other.

9. *Name three physical accomplishments that can be developed in a properly executed golf swing.*
(a) Poise, balance, or good posture.
(b) A sense of rhythm in movement, or coordination.

(c) Ability to use body and hands in generating energy, transmitting and controlling it through the instrument of a golf club.

10. *In checking another player's form list in proper order three things that are essential in the "swing." (This does not refer to the grip or stance but to the stroke itself.)*

(a) Footwork, or proper shifting of weight.

(b) Hand action, or positioning of the club.

(c) The pivot, or turn of the body, which is the motion that actually carries or swings the club back and forth.

11. *Why is the overlapping grip the most natural and effective grip to use in golf?*

Because with this grip the hands can best work toward:

(a) positioning the club correctly,

(b) maintaining that position, and

(c) transmitting to the club through leverage the force created by the body turn.

In referring to force in the golf swing it must always be borne in mind that force is in direct ratio to the speed of clubhead travel, hence a grip that allows free and firm action without any breaking influence is ideal for the golf swing.

12. *What part of the stance, grip, or swing has given you the most difficulty?*

13. *List your suggestions as to how the presentation of material in this course could be improved.*

The last two questions are intended to make the pupils realize that the work is founded on cooperation and mutual understanding, and to make sure that attention is given to all of the pupils' problems.

Answers Guide Program

Excerpts from students' answers give an illuminating cross section of how your instruction is being received.

Not many of the students have had previous golf experience. A few of them have played a few rounds with their fathers and had a few lessons. Others have caddied and a number have hit balls at practice ranges. Those who have had previous experience, you will note, already have picked up bad swing habits that must be corrected. Fortunately, they are not so far advanced that the corrective job is serious. Fortunately too, most young people are fairly responsive to muscle instruction and quite imitative. But when you do get some stubbornly awkward cases I think that the golf instruction makes them more graceful.

There is one great difference between the instruction of adults and younger people. You have to work subtly and persistently to get most adults to relax enough to get good body and arm action. Most young people are so loose they are inclined to be sloppy and inconsistent swingers.

I also found, in the answers to Question 2, that the pupils had a clear idea of the lasting value of golf education. This awareness is made evident not only in the invariably correct answers to the question, but in the class attitude, which is most cooperative and not in the lackadaisical spirit of simply going to class to kill time in fun and get credit for physical education.

All students get the idea that golf is a sport that can increase in its value to the student after he leaves college. I frequently cite cases of young men who were good golfers and for whom the business contacts made through golf resulted in far more earning power in their careers than college stars in other sports have achieved directly, or indirectly, from their athletic activity. Instances, discreetly told, of the valuable social contacts young men and women have made through golf also make an impression on the students.

While thus being coldly realistic, I keep the mental and

physical values of the training before the students and find in the examination answers that the students have been quick to realize the merit of golf training in developing self-control, coordination, and the capacity to adjust one's personality pleasantly to others.

One answer that pleased me, and showed me a value of golf in school work that I'd never realized, was given by a student who said "golf provides a means of relaxation after a steady grind in class." This young man is an intense, high-strung scholar and golf training has been of immediate value to him.

Rule Study Important

The rules of golf are far more interesting than the average golfer ever realizes. So few golfers ever read the rules that there's sometimes a question of what game they're playing.

The basic rule of golf is to *play the ball as it lies.* An old Scotch-born professional once made an amusing comment on the tendency of newer players to deviate from the basic rule. He said, "In Scotland we used to hit the ball around the course; here my pupils want to carry it around."

It is definite that women golfers have done much to promote study and observance of the rules. Women players and officials read the rules, know them, and apply them in getting the fullest interest from the game.

Because high school and college golfers have to do a considerable amount of their competitive play at private clubs where their conduct as guests determines whether or not they will be invited back, it is essential that the instructor see that the pupils are thoroughly conversant with the golf rules and the etiquette that is associated with the rules code.

It is advisable to read the rules in several installments

as part of the golf instruction program and to have question periods on the rules now and then.

The basic rule of "playing the ball as it lies" is, of course, the controlling factor in club design. In further explaining the elements of club design a professional who knows clubs can do an interesting and most helpful job for the students. The pupil must realize that clubs are designed to do specific work in making the shot and that this work relieves the player of the necessity of making physical adjustments for every normal shot.

Questions 5, 6 and 7, of course, are to remind the student that distance and direction are the factors that are mainly controlled by amount of body turn and hand action, respectively. Question 8 is to remind the student of the importance of correct shifting of weight. Answers to these four questions indicate to the instructor the extent to which the pupil understands and has retained the fundamental principles of the swing and how an error of omission accounts for the most common faults of the ordinary golfer.

The answers to questions 9, 10, and 11 show that it is imperative to teach by the routine system because some of the students have a great deal of difficulty in attaining physical poise, rhythm, and coordination and they become tangled and awkward in balance, footwork, hand action, and body turning. The problem of the clumsy youth is a challenge to the physical educator. Yet, by developing some grace, coordination, and "feel" with the golf routine, the instructor helps this type of pupil far beyond the bounds of the game. Incidentally, I have never seen a good golfer, male or female, who wasn't also a good dancer.

As answers to question 12 (What part of the stance, grip or swing has given you the most difficulty?), I want to cite one batch of examination papers as reminders to instructors. Some of these answers disclose that, as much as I have tried to eliminate misunderstandings acquired from previous sketchy association with golf, these misunderstandings continue.

Here are some of the difficulties listed:

Not keeping head steady.
Not keeping left arm straight.
Not breaking wrist at end of swing.
Shifting the body weight forward at beginning of swing.
Shifting of weight from left to right preparatory to swinging.
Weight shift.
The cock of the wrists without stopping.
Making backswing without jerking body and head.
Downswing.
Bringing hands into the swing.
Positioning clubhead on the backswing.
Keeping head down and eye on the ball.
Lifting club away from ball before starting turn of the body.
Pulling with right hand on club before swing has started.
Getting raising effect with right hand while pushing down with left.
Keeping correct wrist position at top of backswing.
Keeping the club straight during swing.
Finding it difficult to follow through.
Shifting weight back to left foot before starting downswing.
Tendency to lose balance.
The grip.
After shifting from left foot to right, having trouble keeping hands over ball.
Changing over from old method.
Downswing (too much independent use of arms).
Too fast on upswing.

REGULAR POSITION
(Normal Straight Shot)

GRIP (regular): left hand on top side of club; left thumb back of shaft at 10:30. Right hand in normal position on club.

STANCE (regular): toes on a line parallel to the direction of the shot.

CLUB: in normal position: shaft tilted forward just slightly so that hands are at a point just above the ball. See dotted line.

BALL: directly opposite left *heel.*

GRIP: left hand brought to a point more in front of shaft. Left thumb at 11:00 o'clock. Right hand also more at top of club.

STANCE: right foot advanced so that body turned slightly towards direction of shot.

CLUB: shaft in more perpendicular position so that hands are above a point behind ball. Note dotted line. Clubface is slightly "toed in" on ball.

BALL: opposite left foot.

GRIP: left hand more on top of shaft; left thumb at 9:00 o'clock. Right hand turned more under shaft.

STANCE (closed): right foot drawn back so body is faced slightly away from line of shot.

CLUB: placed to ball with clubface slightly open and shaft tilted so hands are above a point well ahead of ball. Note dotted line.

BALL: slightly closer to right foot.

Right knee relaxed; giving sitting down effect.
Weight on left foot.
Toes on line parallel to "shot."

Club has been picked up with right hand. Simultaneously, a
downward thrust of left arm, with the left wrist turned
outward or away from body, kicks or sets* the club on
inside of line of shot and also turns the face of club
towards ground.

---

* *To set or cock the club:* Player may set club in a closed position by
tilting shaft inside line of shot, turning clubface toward ground to set it
square with ball, or tilt clubface outside line of shot away from ball or
toward the sky if the reverse effect, or a slice effect is desired.

HOOK SHOT
(Top of swing)

Note face of club pointing to sky. This is the same as keeping the club square to ball throughout the swing.

Note left wrist position: it is straight; not turned under shaft. This has been called the "American Grip Position." "Closed" club at top of swing.

Club will swing from "inside out."

Full turn of body swings the club out and *with* the ball—not across the ball.

SLICE SHOT
(Setting or cocking the club)

This is called the "open" position of club.
Note that shaft is "kicked" to outside line of shot.
Clubface is turned to sky.

SLICE SHOT
(Top of swing)

Shaft is tilted across line of shot.

Clubface is now turned away from ball.

This combination must cause player to swing across the ball and therefore slice.

Club is in "open" position at top of swing.

Player's body turn has almost brought weight back on right
foot.

Ball is above foot level. This situation invariably produces a hook.

Best procedure is to aim to right and "play for the hook."

SIDE-HILL LIE
(Ball below foot position)

Ball is below foot level.

This situation invariably produces a slice.

Best procedure is to aim to left and "play for the slice."

Tendency to take too big a swing on all shots.
Tendency to leave out movements in swing.
Playing ball from a position off left heel.

This examination was given after four lessons in the eight-step procedure and the pupils generally were beginning to exhibit pretty good swings. It will be noted that there was very little difficulty with the grip and taking position to the ball. The difficulties in action were about evenly divided between weight shifting and hand action.

Question 13 (List your suggestions as to how the presentation of materials in this course could be improved.) gave much valuable information for the instructor planning a program for college students, and most of the suggestions probably apply to juniors and seniors in high schools.

To me, the answers indicated the same impatience to learn rapidly that older men and women show. This means there has to be a lively blend of talking instruction, explanation, demonstration, and action by the pupils to maintain interest. The need of more organization and extension of facilities than usually are available was also indicated.

The answers also contained the suggestion that arranging pitching and putting competitions to get action and tests of proficiency into the course is helpful. It's natural for the students to want to see the ball travel far, but it's just this desire that accounts for the fact that few beginners ever learn to be sure of hitting the ball either far or accurately. Consequently, interest in the short game has to be aroused in every possible way.

Students Evaluate the Program

Some of the answers to question 13 give typical student reactions which must be considered in planning the program:

Give more putting practice.

Instead of having nets, have groups on each side of the field driving golf balls to each other.

Get out on a golf course more.

Have a Golf II course under professional supervision on a golf course, with distance and direction training on a driving range.

Discussion of playing on a course.

Book instruction help.

More long hitting. ("I can't tell whether I'm slicing or hooking.")

More work with woods.

Don't have grammar school tactics of "equal competition." Let class select own competitors and do not grade according to competition.

Need personal check-up.

Need more full swing sessions.

Need a golf course for instruction just as much as tennis courts are provided for instruction in tennis.

Need more instruction with different clubs under actual playing conditions.

A lot of demonstrations in which students have opportunity to try the shots and have execution criticized.

Have at least one green on the field where instruction is given.

Use of flags to give more realism to approach practice.

Have an actual game at least once a month with instructor inspecting the form of players.

Instruction should be co-educational.

Small classes to allow more personal instruction.

The answers very plainly indicate that the set-up for most effective school instruction calls for use of outdoor facilities that enable the students to hit long shots that will give them satisfying evidence of progress. The instructor knows it's sound logic to establish good form by work on the short game, but the active young student must hit out balls. A compromise must be made.

When the golf program can be associated with instruction, practice, and play on a course, development is faster. However, lack of course or range facilities or adverse weather conditions limit this outside work, and the instructor has to do the best possible in devising facilities that will advance the instruction and keep students interested by giving them something similar to real playing conditions.

HALL'S 16-WEEK PROGRAM

Ray Hall described a golf teaching plan for schools that his experience determined as very successful. The Hall program, as outlined for the National Golf Foundation follows:

1st Week

Explain to the class the values of golf and the pleasure they may expect to derive from it.

Explain the objects of the game—playing the ball from the tee through the fairway, approaching the green, and finally, putting out.

Discuss the various clubs to be used—their names, the difference in loft and design, and the purpose of each.

Explain the meaning of a few simple golf terms the students will use—such as tee, fairway, apron, green, hazards, cup, hole, turf, and others. It may be advisable to have students make a more complete list of common terms and definitions to be learned or referred to as the work progresses.

2nd Week

Explain and demonstrate the simple fundamental elements that are involved in all swinging strokes—such as the grip, stance, wrist action, backswing, pivot, and follow-through.

Teach the proper grip. Explain its bearing on proper

wrist action and control of the clubface. Describe guides for proper placement of the hands on club. Utilize practice exercises for handling the club and familiarity of the grip.

3rd Week

Pitch-and-run shot played with No. 5 iron or other medium-lofted club. Emphasize the value of short approach shots. Describe its relation to putting and the conditions which make this shot practical.

Explain the fundamentals of this stroke—stance, arm-and-wrist action, position of the ball, pivot, and follow-through. Demonstrate these points.

Practice in unison without balls to develop the stroke.

Actual practice in playing the shots with balls on turf, sand, or other green.

4th Week

Continued practice on pitch-and-run shot, correcting errors, and improving form. These first strokes are very important, because definite habits are being formed. The basic elements of the golf stroke are being developed here, to be carried out to a greater degree as the students progress into longer shots and more complete swings.

Some students will need individual help, and all should be watched carefully during these first days of actual work with the stroke.

Give the students their first performance test in this shot. Draw one or more circles around the cup, allowing so many points for holing out, a fewer number in the smaller circle and so on, according to the number of circles. Give each student a certain number of shots and total their score, posting the class winner and the class average. Every golfer must learn to perform before others, maintaining poise, concentration, and relaxation. Do not stress the value of good scoring as much as that of gaining competitive experience.

5th Week

The pitch or chip shot, played with a No. 7 iron. Compare the No. 5 and No. 7 irons, explaining the difference in results obtained, and the conditions calling for this type of shot. Show similarity of these two styles of short approaches in the general fundamentals and execution, but a different action of the ball because of a more lofted club.

Explain the principle of backspin and how it is accomplished, and why, at times, this type of shot is valuable. Practice this style of approach.

6th Week

Continued practice in the pitch shot, with improvised hazards as an incentive to acquire proper elevation of the ball.

Second performance test in short approach shots, this time permitting the student to make his own selection between the No. 5 and No. 7 iron. Comparison with scores of the first test will probably show improvement, and this fact should be commented on to the class.

Emphasize again that the important thing just now is a good fundamental stroke, and that scoring is secondary and will be developed through practice.

7th Week

The putting stroke. Explain the grip, stance, function of the hands, wrists, and arms, and the mechanics of the stroke.

Impress upon the students the importance of putting and the percentage of putts to the entire score; also the relation of putting to short approaches, and the importance of the short game as a whole.

Practice actually putting strokes on the green or with putting cups and rugs.

8th Week

Continued putting practice. If possible conduct an eighteen or thirty-six hole putting contest on a regular grass putting green, giving the students practice and experience on an actual putting surface.

Another interesting event is to pair the class into teams, allowing one member of the team to play the short approaches and the other to putt out the balls for an aggregate score. This will emphasize the relationship of good approach shots to putting. If desired, the order can then be reversed, giving all students more practice in both shots, thus showing any weaknesses.

Putting permits more individuality of form than any other stroke, and here again the instructor must give individual help so that each student may develop the most natural style while adhering to the basic fundamentals of a sound putting stroke.

9th Week

Long approach shots. In the short approach shots the students have learned the proper grip and have developed in a smaller degree the elements of stance, back-swing, pivot, and follow-through.

In playing the longer approaches these elements are developed into the longer strokes, such as the half and three-quarter swing, changing the stance, and increasing the back stroke and body action as required.

These half and three-quarter strokes are played with both the No. 7 and No. 5 iron into the nets or curtain. Because these two clubs are used for all distances of approach, the student must learn to alter his swing to meet the required distance to the green. It may be a full swing or any part of it. Through the half and three-quarter strokes the student will be developing his form and the use of fundamentals that will eventually make up his full swing.

10th Week

Explain all the elements that make up the full stroke—function of the wrists and arms, full pivot, back stroke, balance, and finish of the swing.

Practice exercises in unison to develop pivot and balance.

Club-swinging exercises in unison to a rhythmic count will develop smooth, well-timed strokes.

The full shots have two objectives—distance and accuracy. These cannot be obtained consistently without good form and a sound swing. The students should develop these essentials through swinging exercises before attempting to play actual shots into the net. This week can well be spent in the preliminary work of developing a good swing.

11th Week

No. 2 iron shots.

This week is spent practicing full shots with the long irons. In addition to the points previously stressed, the elements of power and timing are involved.

Study illustrations or charts showing form in the full strokes.

The students have now reached the enticing part of the game of golf, and will need no encouragement to practice.

12th Week

Continued practice with long irons.

Another performance test will be interesting and valuable. Paint a bulls-eye with circles around it on the back curtain, or hang up a separate target curtain in the net, scoring similar to that in the approach shots.

13th Week

Wood shots. Since the strokes with the long irons and woods embody the same general fundamentals, the routine is similar to that with the irons.

Explain the difference between tee and fairway shots with woods.

Practice driving with ball teed up; brassie shots played off mat.

The work as outlined here calls for use of a minimum of clubs, hence the suggestion of the brassie as the only wood club used. Beginners, and especially women, have trouble getting the ball up well off the tee, and many have better success driving with a brassie. It is the all-purpose wood.

14th Week

Continued practice on the wood shots, with further analysis of the mechanics of the full swing.

Analyze the causes and remedies for the common errors, such as topping, slicing, hooking, pulling, and pushing.

Strive for good form and control before attempting maximum power and distance.

Performance test with the wood club similar to that given with the irons.

15th Week

Review the short game, approaching, and putting.

After intensive work with the long strokes, there may be some confusion about the fundamental points and actions involved in playing the various shots. Some students will have forgotten some of the important points in playing these short approaches and putts. This review will serve as a final checkup on the short game.

16th Week

This last week with the class should be given over to a study of the common rules and etiquette of golf and the procedure of actual play on the course.

Explain the method of scoring in both match and stroke play, how to figure and use handicaps, with the use of a score card.

Many of these students will soon be playing their first game of golf, and the better they are prepared to meet the actual playing conditions, the more pleasure will be theirs.

Explain that in the work thus far, the students have only secured a foundation of the basic fundamentals upon which to build future progress. There is still much to be learned by actual play and experience on the golf course. Further progress will depend upon their individual efforts, continued instruction, application, study, and practice.

If the work as outlined here, or modified to meet local conditions, has been carried out with competent instruction and with sincere effort on the part of the students, they will be well-prepared to start out in a game that will afford them a lifetime of enjoyment and benefit. The school and the instructor may be justly proud of having made this opportunity possible, and of the part they have taken in increasing golf in schools.

COORDINATE WITH OUTSIDE PLAY

In every locality where there is a public course there should be close coordination between instruction at the school and at the course. The professional at the course will be of invaluable help to the school P. E. staff in arranging this tie-up and in planning extensive use of the facilities of the public recreation facility he directs. At some of these public courses reduced rates for high school or local college students are made during days and hours when play generally is not heavy.

At Long Beach, California, George Lake, the public course professional, arranged a program for high school students that is considered a model of its kind. In other localities public course professionals have done excellent jobs of this nature. A number of privately owned daily-fee courses also have professional cooperation and student reduced rates are available for the development of golf.

In the case of private clubs quite a few of them allow some high school- or college-student play at times when member use of the courses isn't heavy. To preserve this privilege students must be very careful about observing the etiquette of golf and must be under the supervision of a member of the school P. E. staff. The extent to which these courtesies are extended depends mainly on the students, and their performance is governed by the training and supervision they receive.

Entry sheets, promotion material, and medals are available as prizes for school tournaments without cost from the National Golf Foundation which, in association with the Professional Golfers' Association Junior Promotion Committees, is steadily engaged in extending golf education in schools.

Much of the basic plan for school instruction can be employed in organizing and conducting classes of employees at offices and factories and at YMCA's, YWCA's and other youth and general community centers.

Index